Interpretationshilfen

A Lesson Before Dying

Ernest J. Gaines

Cornelsen

Patrick Charles

A Lesson Before Dying · Interpretationshilfe

Verlagsredaktion
Neil Porter

Umschlagdesign
Klein & Halm Grafikdesign, Berlin

Technische Umsetzung
Antje Kanniga, Köln

Bilder: S. 5, 13, 85, 91: © Bettmann/CORBIS; S. 10: National Geographic/ Getty Images/Willard R. Culver; S. 31, 61, 65, 69: pwe Kinoarchiv Hamburg/defd Deutscher Fernsehdienst; S. 89: Getty Images/Michael Ochs Archives; S. 92: © JP Laffont/Sygma/Corbis; S. 111 (links): Getty Images/Transcendental Graphics; S. 111 (rechts): Getty Images/Keystone

www.cornelsen.de

1. Auflage, 2. Druck 2011

Druck: CS-Druck CornelsenStürtz, Berlin

ISBN: 978-3-589-04625-6

Inhalt gedruckt auf säurefreiem Papier aus nachhaltiger Forstwirtschaft.

Contents

All page and line references are to the Cornelsen edition of *A Lesson Before Dying* (Berlin: Cornelsen Verlag, 2009); ISBN 978-3-06-032185-8.

Ernest J. Gaines

Ernest J. Gaines was born in 1933 on the River Lake plantation in Louisiana, near the town of New Roads. The eldest of twelve children, he was raised by his aunt in the old slave quarters on the plantation. His father was a sharecropper. Sharecroppers were agricultural laborers who raised crops on farm plots owned by large landowners. The landowner supplied the sharecropper with the land, housing, tools, and seeds. The planter also retained legal rights to the crop. After harvest, the sharecropper would be paid a share of the produce instead of cash wages. Typically he would receive one-third to one-half of the crops. Gaines himself had to work in the fields as a child. He was educated in the church on the plantation during the half-year in which the children would not have to work picking cotton. He went on to study at a Catholic school in the area before moving to California with his mother and step-father.

His first novel was written when he was 17, and although it was rejected, he later re-wrote it and had it published as *Catherine Carmier* (1964). He studied at San Francisco State University, graduating with a degree in Literature in 1957. After spending two years in the US army, he won a scholarship to the prestigious Stanford University. Gaines has divided his time since the 1980s between San Francisco in California and Lafayette in Louisiana, where he teaches a Creative Writing workshop at the University of Louisiana.

Gaines's career as a writer began with the publication of the short story *"The Turtles"* in 1956, which was published in a magazine at his university. He has had numerous other short stories published, and has written nine novels. His themes and topics are for the most part inspired by African-American life in Louisiana, dealing with issues of race, racism, identity in the context of family and place, social changes, and generational conflicts. Many of his works are taught in schools and universities around the world, and several have been adapted for the stage, cinema and television.

A Lesson Before Dying is set in a fictional Cajun community, called Bayonne, in Louisiana in the 1940s. It can be broadly characterized as a historical novel about racial segregation and the death penalty. Since its publication in 1993 it has become Gaines's most famous and acclaimed novel. As with all of Gaines's writing, the novel is firmly rooted in the world he experienced – the setting of the book is similar to the plantation on which he grew up, the narrator's aunt Lou is similar to Gaines's own Aunt Augusteen, who raised him, and the narrator's work as a school teacher, as well as his ambivalent attitude to his home and upbringing, mirrors Gaines's own experience.

The issues raised in the novel remain relevant: as with all serious historical fiction, the past is used here to reflect the present. The effects of slavery, racial segregation, and discrimination are shown in the novel in their pre-Civil Rights movement context, but Gaines's intention in the novel is not bound to one particular era. The essential issue of dignity in life and death is timeless.

Synopsis

The story is set in a small town in Louisiana in 1948. Convicted of the murder of a white shopkeeper, Jefferson is sentenced to death in the electric chair. His godmother Miss Emma is shocked that his defence lawyer calls him a "*hog*", and asks Grant Wiggins, the nephew of her best friend Lou, to help teach Jefferson to die like a man.

Grant is a schoolteacher with a university education, who hates life in the segregated South, but cannot bring himself to leave. He lives with his aunt Lou and has a relationship with a teacher from town, a married woman called Vivian. He is sceptical about what he can do for Jefferson, but agrees (under pressure from his aunt and from Emma) to ask for permission to visit Jefferson in jail.

They visit the plantation owner, Henri Pichot, in whose house both Emma and Lou worked all their lives, and where Grant spent a lot of his childhood, to ask him to ask the sheriff for permission for Grant to visit Jefferson, which the sheriff does.

The visits are extremely difficult. Jefferson is depressed and rejects Grant's help. Grant finds himself having to rely more and more on Vivian for support as he grows slowly closer to Jefferson. He becomes involved in disagreements with the preacher Reverend Ambrose, who believes that all Jefferson needs is religious faith. During this time (from autumn 1948 to Easter 1949) a number of things happen: Vivian visits Grant and meets Lou, Grant prepares the Christmas program with his school which is dedicated to Jefferson, Grant becomes friendly with a white deputy at the jail, Grant buys a radio for Jefferson. Most importantly Grant gives Jefferson a notebook in which to write down his thoughts. Grant also talks to Jefferson about heroes and myths, and the importance of doing things for other people.

The last chapters contain the contents of Jefferson's notebook, in which we learn that the black people all come and visit him, so Jefferson is aware of his role in the community. On the day of Jefferson's execution, Grant has his pupils pray for Jefferson, and he has the feeling when it is all over that, in a way, he has succeeded in helping Jefferson become the man his godmother wanted him to be when he went to his death.

The Story

Chapter One

The trial and sentence

The first chapter describes Jefferson's trial. Grant, the novel's narrator, is not present at the trial but says that he was *"as much as anyone else was there"* (p. 1, l. 3).

Jefferson's version of the crime is described: He was picked up by Brother and Bear on his way to the White Rabbit Bar and Lounge, where they had tried to buy alcohol from the store owner, Alcee Gropé. When Gropé refused to give them alcohol on credit because he knew they didn't have any money and would not be able to pay off their credit, Bear approached him in a threatening manner: Gropé seized a gun and begun shooting; and by the time it was over, Jefferson was the only person left alive. Traumatized by the events, Jefferson was unable to leave and drank a bottle of whiskey. He then stole money from the cash register and was about to leave when two white men walked into the store.

The prosecutor then gives his version of events, in which Jefferson and the two other dead men had gone there with the intention of robbing and killing old Gropé.

The defence argues that Jefferson was in the wrong place at the wrong time, and that Jefferson is largely innocent. The defence lawyer's plea is given in full. The lawyer's case is based around the idea that Jefferson is basically too stupid and subhuman – he calls him a *"hog"*

This section in the novel is important, as it introduces the racist thinking which provokes Miss Emma to ask Grant to visit Jefferson in prison.

and a "*thing*" – to have been a guilty participant in the crime.

The jury reaches the verdict that Jefferson is guilty of robbery and murder in the first degree. The judge sentences Jefferson to death by electrocution.

Chapter Two

Miss Emma's wish

On the afternoon of the day of the sentencing, Grant comes home from the school where he works as a teacher. His aunt Tante Lou is there with Miss Emma. Grant feels uncomfortable and tries to get away, arguing that he has to go to Bayonne, but Tante Lou insists that he talk with Miss Emma.

The relationship between Grant and his aunt is not an easy one.

Miss Emma explains – indirectly – what she expects from Grant ("*I want a man to go to that chair, on his own two feet*", p. 14, ll. 25–6). Grant is unwilling to get involved, but his aunt ignores him and insists that he accompany her and Emma to the plantation owner, Henri Pichot, who is brother-in-law to Sheriff Guidry. Grant's complaint that there is nothing he can do now for Jefferson, that he is already dead, is ignored. The three of them get ready to leave for Pichot's house.

Chapter Three

Visiting Henri Pichot

Grant drives the two old women to Henri Pichot's plantation house, where they enter through the side door – reserved for servants and delivery men. Grant points out to Tante Lou that she had never wanted him to use this "*back door*" again to

Blacks were rarely invited indoors, and if so, had to enter through the back door.

enter the house, but she reminds him that today is not a typical day. They are met at the door by Inez Lane, Pichot's maid. She tells them that Henri is talking to someone in the library, and has them wait in the kitchen. Inez announces them, and Henri and his friend Louis Rougon, a banker, come to the kitchen to hear what Miss Emma has to say.

Even after the end of slavery blacks continued to work in the houses of the former plantation owners.

The descendant of the plantation owner is still seen as the person blacks must deal with.

Henry Pichot is obviously annoyed at the interruption, and is hesitant when it becomes clear that Miss Emma wishes to ask a favor of him. The casual arrogance of the plantation owner is evident in his unspoken commands to the maid and by the fact that he does not offer Jefferson's exhausted old godmother a seat in the kitchen.

Miss Emma asks him to speak to the Sheriff about allowing Grant to visit Jefferson in jail and *"make him know he's not a hog, he's a man"* (p.21, ll. 16–17). Pichot obviously doesn't want to get involved, but feels a kind of commitment to both Miss Emma and Tante Lou for their many years of service in his house. He listens to Emma's demands and speaks briefly to Grant. Pichot is unimpressed by Grant's answers and has no interest in Miss Emma's plan: he suggests that it would be best to leave the visiting to Reverend Ambrose. Emma knows that the Reverend will be seeing to Jefferson to help prepare him for death – in a religious sense. But what she wants is for him also to be prepared as a man. Pichot and Louis Rougon are astonished by her words. Pichot can't believe that she wants to expend any more energy on Jefferson, who is guilty of murder, and will be executed. He has not understood Emma's wish: *"I'm not begging for his life no more; that's over. I just want to see him die like a man."* (p. 23, ll. 6–7) She is insistent, constantly reminding Henri Pichot of her service to his household since before his birth. He relents, impatient to get away from the difficult and awkward situation. The old woman is persistent to the last: finally the two white men retreat to the library and Grant leaves with his aunt and Jefferson's godmother.

Chapter Four

Grant meets with Vivian

Grant drives his aunt and Miss Emma back to Tante Lou's house. He refuses her offer of food, thereby hurting her feelings, and drives to the Rainbow Club in Bayonne, where he calls his girlfriend Vivian Baptiste and asks her to come to the club to see him. This section includes a description of the layout and make-up of the town of Bayonne, showing how the town is divided

Grant´s girlfriend Vivian is not known to his aunt or the rest of the quarter.

between white and "*colored*" areas and establishments.

Grant is apparently a regular at the Rainbow Club, where the proprietors, Joe and Thelma Clairborne, run a combined bar and café. Grant eats and has a brandy while he waits for Vivian. When she arrives she makes an impression, as she is a very beautiful woman. They talk, and Grant asks her if she would leave the area with him right now. She can't, as she is separated from her husband, with whom she has two children, and is waiting for a divorce. Grant's frustration with his life in Bayonne and annoyance at Miss Emma's request leads him to complain bitterly about his life. Vivian calms him and they dance. Vivian says that she wants him to go to see Jefferson if the sheriff allows it. They arrange to meet at the weekend in Baton Rouge, a nearby city, as they cannot be alone together in Bayonne. They finish their drinks and leave the bar.

Sexual relations outside of marriage are considered immoral and would harm her attempt to get a divorce and lower his reputation as a teacher.

Chapter Five

Grant's school

In this chapter we are introduced to the school where Grant teaches, and to his pupils. The school is improvised in a church, with one small table for the teacher and benches for the pupils to sit on and work at. In this chapter we see Grant at work with the children, and see more of the narrator's less sympathetic nature. He is impatient, intimidating, sarcastic, and, at times, cruel. His cynical attitude towards his pupils and lack of respect for their efforts further highlights his deep resentment towards his life in Bayonne: this is not what he wants to do for the rest of his life.

This chapter reveals the inadequacy of black education and how frustrated Grant feels at being unable to change anything.

An example of a rural black school in the South

The chapter begins with the class pledging allegiance to the US flag outside the church-schoolroom. Grant then asks his pupils to recite Bible verses, during which he thinks about the rest of his day in school. He describes his school, the age range (6 to 14) of his pupils, and the furnishing of the classroom. We learn how he organizes the teaching, using the older children to teach the youngest while he teaches the middle grades and then spends the last couple of hours in the day with the older children. While organizing and directing his class, Grant is thinking about the problems with his aunt: she is angry with him and avoids speaking to him. His guilt and irritation about the situation at home makes him short-tempered with his pupils: he hits one of the boys in his class with a ruler, twice, simply for calculating with his fingers instead of in his head. The pupils are terrified of Grant, fearful of both his vicious sarcasm and of being struck with the ruler he carries around the classroom.

Grant walks around outside the school, and the reader is given an impression of the poverty of the black settlement that can be seen from the school. Going back into the building through the back door, he sees one of his pupils playing with an insect instead of reading, and strikes him over the head with the ruler. The boy starts crying, the rest of the class is scared.

Grant then explains to the class how Jefferson is going to be executed. Although he knows that all the pupils are aware of the impending execution, he goes into some detail, shocking them. He then tells them what Jefferson's aunt expects him to do – and draws a parallel to what he is trying to do with his class. One of the girls he had disciplined begins crying: Jefferson is her cousin. Grant knows this but does not apologize to her or show any sympathy.

The sense of community is strong: see how even the children are involved in Jefferson's fate.

He sets the class to write a test. That afternoon, Henri Pichot's handyman, Farrell Jarreau, comes to the school to tell Grant that Pichot will see him that evening, concerning Jefferson.

Chapter Six

A meeting with the sheriff at Pichot's

Grant enters Mr. Pichot's house through the back door, and finds Inez, who has been crying, in the kitchen. The sheriff, Sam Guidry, will be arriving shortly. Inez tells Grant that Mr. Pichot and Louis Rougon are discussing a bet as to whether or not Grant will be able to *"get [Jefferson] ready to die"* (p.41, l.21).

Grant is kept waiting in the kitchen for nearly two and a half hours. Inez offers him food, but his pride stops him from eating at Pichot's kitchen table. The sheriff's wife, Edna Guidry, comes to

This treatment is intended to humiliate Grant.

the kitchen to get more bourbon and make small talk with Grant. When Inez finally tells him that the men will soon be coming, she lets him know that, although Henri Pichot is against allowing Grant to visit Jefferson, Edna Guidry has put in a word for him.

Eventually they come to the kitchen to see Grant: Henri Pichot, Sam Guidry, Louis Rougon, and "*another fat man*" (p.45, l.20), all carrying their glasses of brandy. Grant is unsure of the situation, torn between acting as the educated man of intelligence that he is, but which he believes they would interpret as an insult, or acting like "*the nigger that I was supposed to be*" (p.46, l.1), which would have been an insult to himself. He can see in their faces that they have made up their minds already: but the sheriff asks him anyway what he wants. They go through the motions of talking about what Grant can do for Jefferson, and Sam Guidry makes it clear that he disapproves of both Grant's intelligence ("*Maybe you're just a little too smart for your own good.*" (p.48, ll.5–6)) and the nature of the request ("*But my wife thinks different*" (p.47, ll.33–4)). He is suspicious, and doesn't believe that anything will come of the visits, except maybe for aggravating Jefferson. He agrees however to allow Grant to visit Jefferson in jail, with a few minor conditions as to when he can go and what he may bring into jail with him; the visits are to begin in two weeks' time. Grant is then dismissed, and leaves.

Note how the white men go to the kitchen rather than let Grant go to the living quarters.

Chapter Seven

A visit from the school superintendent

Grant is warned that the local superintendent for schools will soon be visiting. Every day Grant makes sure that the children are clean and dressed correctly, and he makes one pupil stand outside the school every day to keep an eye out for cars. On a Thursday afternoon the man finally arrives. He is a short, fat man called Dr. Joseph Morgan. He fails to remember Grant's name, even when reminded that it is Wiggins and not Higgins, and seems unimpressed by the school. Grant's assistant, Irene Cole, is in charge of the children during the visit, something they had been rehearsing for days.

In this chapter we see how institutionalized segregation works in the education system.

Dr. Joseph begins inspecting the school. He examines the children's hands, asks which Bible verses they know, and asks them questions about grammar, math, and geography. He also inspects their hands and teeth. Seeing this, Grant is reminded of stories of slave owners who would do the same, and of cattle dealers who did the same with horses and cattle. Dr. Joseph then lectures the children on nutrition and recommends "*good exercise*" (p. 55, l. 17), i.e. picking cotton, gathering potatoes, and so on. Grant feels ashamed for having drilled the children so correctly.

He tries to ask Dr. Joseph for more material for the school – books, chalk, paper, pencils, even a heater – but Dr. Joseph is not interested. When Grant insists, the superintendent gets annoyed with him, and tells him to emphasize hygiene. He also tells him to get the children to harvest the pecan trees on the school grounds which they can then sell.

Chapter Eight

Grant reflects on education

During the next week two men bring the winter firewood for the school. The wood has to be chopped up by the school children. Grant watches the boys chopping the wood up that afternoon, and wonders what he is doing – the boys he is teaching are no different from the two uneducated old men who had brought the wood. He thinks about earlier students of his who had gone back to work in the fields, or gone to the cities where they had been killed or sent to prison. He recalls his mulatto teacher, Matthew Antoine, who had watched Grant and other pupils chopping wood, and had warned them that they would either die violently or be brought down to the level of beasts. He had warned them to run – he hadn't, and they could sense his self-hatred because of it. His presence reminded them that there is no freedom in how and where they live. Antoine saw that Grant was different: that he would learn and move on to better things. Grant senses that Antoine hated him for his potential, and also for his blackness. After Grant returned from college, he could feel Antoine's contempt for him for having returned to the area. He had told Grant that his work as a teacher would be pointless, that he won't be able to *"scrape away the blanket of ignorance that has been plastered and replastered over those brains in the past three hundred years."* (p.62, ll.20–2)

Antoine serves as a warning to Grant as to how he might become.

Grant needed the older man's cynical statements, which no one else would express. He listened to Antoine's self-contempt, his self-definition as a Creole – *"Do you know what a Creole is? A lying cowardly bastard."* (p.63, ll.14–15) – which allowed him in the racist South to feel superior to the blacks, despite being himself looked down upon by white society. Antoine repeatedly told Grant to run away and abandon the hopeless situation in the South. Grant says that he wants to learn about life, but Antoine tells him that there is nothing to be found here but ignorance. Grant remembers having visited Antoine shortly before he died in 1942. He had told the old man that he was now a teacher in the school. Antoine had told him: *"It doesn't matter anymore. […] Just do the best you can. But it won't matter."* (p.64, ll.21–3)

Chapter Nine

The first visit to Jefferson in jail

On the day of his first visit to Jefferson in jail in Bayonne, Grant leaves school and picks up Miss Emma. She has a basket with her. Grant's aunt is not coming with them to the jail, and she and Miss Emma finish their conversation as Grant waits. They know that he disapproves of the enterprise, and he is sulky: *"I refused to look into the mirror at them"* (p.65, ll.13–14).

They drive the 13 miles to Bayonne in silence. They arrive at the courthouse at 2 o'clock. Miss Emma tells the two deputies that she has come to visit Jefferson, and that she has brought food and clean clothes with her. The younger deputy – Paul Bonin – seems to Grant to be *"pretty decent"* (p.67, l.30). The other deputy *"didn't look decent at all"* (p.67, l.31) – there is a mutual feeling of dislike, but there is nothing Grant can do about it. The deputy explains the sheriff's rules again – no cutlery, pins, knives, razor blades. He seems to be implying that Jefferson might commit suicide, which Miss Emma finds impossible to believe.

Grant and Miss Emma are led by the young deputy Paul to Jefferson's cell. They are taken through the office area, then upstairs to the area where the jail cells are – white and black on one floor, although in different sections. As they pass the cells, the prisoners ask for money or cigarettes.

Jefferson is by himself at the end of the cellblock, lying on his bed. The deputy tells them that he must lock them in the cell, and that he will return within an hour.

Jefferson doesn't acknowledge Emma or Grant. He lies on his bed staring at the ceiling. Grant and Emma remain standing as there is no place to sit in the cell. Emma tries to talk to Jefferson, but he refuses to talk with them.

Jefferson's rejection of other people is a sign of his rejection of his humanity.

When she tries to give him some food he speaks for the first time. He says that nothing matters. Emma tries to get him to explain, but he repeats that nothing matters, and talks about his death.

Paul returns to let them out of the cell. Jefferson is silent and unresponsive. Miss Emma is upset, and Paul indicates to Grant that he should embrace the old woman and comfort her.

Chapter Ten

Grant learns he will go alone to visit to Jefferson.

The next two visits are much like the first: Grant drives Miss Emma to the courthouse, Jefferson refuses to talk with them or eat the food his godmother has brought, and Miss Emma ends up in tears.

On the day of the fourth visit, Grant goes to pick up Miss Emma. His aunt tells him that Miss Emma isn't able to go as she is ill, but insists he goes alone. Grant suspects that she is nowhere near as ill as she is pretending to be. Grant is suddenly struck by the realization that everything up to now had been in preparation for his being sent on his own to see Jefferson.

Grant protests to his aunt that she is now stripping him of everything for which she had had him educated. He lists the things he has experienced since this whole thing started – humiliation at Pichot's house; having to wait for hours in the kitchen like a house servant; the treatment he must endure at the jail. These are all the things he and his aunt wanted him to escape from. Bitterly, he says that his old teacher, Antoine, had told him that if he stayed here, he would be broken down *"to the nigger I was born to be"* (p. 77, l. 1). Grant says that he hadn't expected his aunt to help the whites do it.

The fact that they want Grant to visit Jefferson is a sign of their belief in him as a teacher and leader.

His humiliation and anger move Miss Emma to tears, although his aunt remains firm. Miss Emma apologizes to him for aiding the white people in humiliating him, for imposing such a burden on him. She says that she wishes there were someone else she could call on to help – but there is no one else.

Chapter Eleven

Grant visits Jefferson by himself.

When Grant arrives at the courthouse, Sheriff Sam Guidry is in the office. He remembers Grant. He orders Paul to search Grant and check the basket of food, as always. The sheriff asks Grant if he still believes that he can teach Jefferson anything.

Jefferson is sitting this time in his cell. Grant asks him if he is hungry. Jefferson asks him if he has brought corn. Grant is confused, but Jefferson says *"That's what hogs eat."* (p. 80, l. 3). Jefferson then tries to show that he is a hog and not a human. Grant asks Jefferson if he is trying to hurt him, and wonders if Jefferson doesn't want him to come any more. He points out that Sheriff Guidry doesn't want him to come either, and questions whether Jefferson wants the white man to win.

Jefferson refuses to say anything, but Grant is unwilling to call for the deputy and leave before the allotted time is up. He fears that that would give Sheriff Guidry a reason to stop the visits, if he had the impression that Grant and Jefferson were not getting along. So Grant sits and waits for the hour to pass. When the deputy returns, Grant asks Jefferson if there is anything he would like to tell Miss Emma. He repeats again that he will tell the old woman how much Jefferson had enjoyed her food.

Grant is caught between rejection by a black man and the fear of losing credibility with the whites.

Chapter Twelve

Grant visits Vivian again.

After leaving the jail, Grant is unsure about what to tell Miss Emma about the visit. He feels he has to lie to her, as the truth would hurt her too much. He drives to the Rainbow Club to give himself time and space to think about it.

The bar is nearly empty, with just a couple of men discussing baseball. Grant orders a beer and sits alone, half-listening to the baseball talk. The old men are talking about a Brooklyn Dodgers player, Jackie Robinson. The men at the bar seem to remember everything this player had ever done.

Grant thinks about the time when the most discussed and loved sportsman among the black community was the boxer, Joe Louis. He recalls how everyone was depressed when Louis lost to the German boxer Max Schmeling, as they felt as

The first black heroes emerged in sport.

though there was nothing left of which they could be proud. Even a preacher at the time asked his congregation to have faith that David (Louis) would meet Goliath (Schmeling) again. The next fight between the two took place when Grant was 17. Everyone in the black quarter followed the fight on the radio. When Louis beat Schmeling the quarter went wild with rejoicing. Grant remembers that, after the fight, "*we held our heads higher than any people on earth had ever done for any reason*" (p.85, ll.23–4).

Then Grant recalls something else – a little Irishman from his time at university. The Irishman had been lecturing at white universities, but had also been engaged to lecture at the blacks-only university Grant was attending at the time. He gave a lecture on famous modern Irish writers, none of whom Grant had never heard of. He lectured in particular about Joyce's short story "*Ivy Day in the Committee Room*", in which men talk about the Irish nationalist politician Parnell. He described the story as being universal – beyond race and beyond class.

After the lecture, Grant finally found a copy of James Joyce's *The Dubliners* (the collection containing the short story). Grant read the story many times but was unable to find the "*universality*" the Irish lecturer had spoken of. It was only years later that he understood it – it is the way the characters in the story talk about their heroes and their dead. These memories have the same unifying, focusing effect on the Irish characters as Joe Louis had on Grant's community in his youth, and as Jackie Robinson has now.

Every culture and race needs its heroes to look up to.

But Grant's recollections are sidetracked again, and he thinks about Jefferson in his cell. But he wants to think only of pleasant things, so he thinks of Vivian. As it is Friday he wants to find her and persuade her to go away with him for the weekend. And then he thinks how much he wants to just leave with her, for good, and never come back.

He leaves the Rainbow Club and heads to Vivian's school. In this district in Bayonne, everyone knows everyone else's business. Vivian is in her classroom checking papers. On the blackboard there are simple English sentences and their French translations. He erases them and writes instead "*Je t'aime*" and "*I love you*". When she returns and sees it, Vivian worries that someone else might see it.

Grant tries to persuade her to leave with him for the weekend, alone – to New Orleans or Baton Rouge. She says she can't because of her children. Grant says that Dora can look after them; Vivian points out that they have arranged to meet Peggy in the Rainbow Club that night. Grant insists that they should just forget everything and everyone, and go. After a momentary hesitation, Vivian says no. She fears that that would give her husband an excuse to take the children from her.

Neither of them enjoys the current arrangement, in which they visit friends in order to be able to sleep together, never spending the whole night together, but Vivian says she can't take the chance of staying away all night, in case her estranged husband hears about it.

Grant tells her of Jefferson's behavior in the jail cell. He tells her that he has to go and see Miss Emma, but cannot face it. He says he wants to just run away. She tells him that he loves "*them*" more than he hates "*this place*" (p. 91, ll. 3–4). He's not sure himself if it is love or cowardice which is keeping him here. He has relatives in California, so he could move there. Vivian tells him that this is all they have. He says he wants more. Grant erases his writing from the blackboard. Vivian then writes "*Je t'aimerais toujours*" in its place. Grant asks her if she is not worried that someone else will see it – she tells him that everyone knows already that they are in love.

Chapter Thirteen

Determination Sunday

On Determination Sunday (the third Sunday in every month, in which the church congregation sing hymns and tell "*where they were determined to spend eternity*", p. 93, ll. 13–14) Tante Lou goes to church without talking to Grant. He had told her once, after returning from university, that he no longer believed – and that he would leave again if she tried to force him to go to church. Since then she has left him in peace, but refuses to look at him when she goes to church.

Grant finds it difficult to concentrate on correcting schoolwork. He thinks about the previous Friday, when after having returned from Bayonne, he found Tante Lou, Miss Emma and the Reverend Ambrose at home. They asked him how Jefferson was and Grant replied that he was alright and that they talked a little. He told them that he had visited his girlfriend in town. Tante Lou accused him of having spent all his time with his girlfriend. The Reverend Ambrose asked him what he thought, "*deep down*", about how Jefferson was, and what was in his head. Grant said that he couldn't know what was deep inside someone else's head.

Ambrose asked if Grant thought that Jefferson was aware of the significance, the gravity, of what it was all about. He asked Grant about Jefferson's soul. Grant was able to retreat into his atheism: *"I don't know anything about the soul, Reverend Ambrose."* (p.96, l.19)

Grant feels superior to Reverend Ambrose, as the latter is uneducated and has no grasp of theology. Grant feels that, as an educated man and a teacher, he is better equipped than Reverend Ambrose to discuss complex, abstract matters.

The Reverend asked him if they had discussed God during the visit. Grant said they didn't *"get around to that"* (p.96, l.28). Grant knew that the Reverend disapproved of this, especially as Jefferson was going to die soon. Grant pointed out that he felt that that was more the Reverend's territory. The Reverend announced that he, Miss Emma and Tante Lou would be visiting Jefferson on Monday. He asked Grant what they might bring for Jefferson – Grant tells them food and clean clothes. The Reverend asked about bringing Jefferson a Bible. Grant said that that would be *"nice"*.

Now, on the Sunday morning, he listens to them all singing in the church, thinking about how many years he had listened to and participated in these services – up until his last year at university. He can't isolate one single factor which had shaken his faith. By and large, he had had no time for anything else except studying. He had wanted to leave Louisiana, as his old teacher Antoine had recommended. He had visited his parents, who live in California, while at university, but had returned to his aunt in Louisiana. Since then, he says, he feels that he had been *"running in place"* – *"unable to accept what used to be my life, unable to leave it."* (p.97, ll.26–7)

Throughout the novel there is a tension between the man of religion and the man of education, with both looking down on the other. By the end, it is clear that both men have shown courage.

A car pulls up and someone approaches the house. It turns out to be Vivian, who has never come to his aunt's house before.

Chapter Fourteen

Vivian and Grant

Vivian says that she spontaneously decided to visit him. She has left her children in Dora's care. Grant apologizes for the house, which is poor. Vivian tries to be nice about things, commenting nicely on the photos of Grant's parents, and describing it as "*rustic*" and "*pastoral*" (p. 100, ll. 6, 9) – both adjectives which apparently, for Grant, have more negative than positive connotations.

They embrace, feeling and knowing that they love each other. They walk through the small house and drink coffee in the kitchen. Vivian tells Grant that he ought to find some occupation for himself on Sundays, which he considers to be the saddest day in the week. She suggests he go to church – he doesn't answer. She says: "*I know you believe […]. You don't want to, but I know you do.*" (p. 101, ll. 18–19) He replies that the only thing he believes in is his love for her.

After finishing their coffee, they leave the house for a walk. Everything is quiet outside – the locals are all either in church or indoors at home. No one can be seen working or outside. They cross the railroad tracks and pass through the loading areas where the sugar cane was prepared and boxed for transportation. They pass by the plantation cemetery, where Grant's ancestors have been buried for centuries. Grant tells Vivian that his people had worked these fields since the days of slavery. He cuts a piece of sugar cane for her as they walk through the fields. Just before the field

The implication here is that nothing has really changed in race relations over the centuries.

gives way to the swampland beyond, they stop under a pecan tree and sit down. Vivian asks him if he wants to make love to her here and now, in the field.

Afterwards, lying together in the field, she says that she thinks that something might have happened – that she feels different. Grant, knowing that she means that she thinks she may have just conceived, is not overjoyed. He is depressed by the idea of his child – whom he assumes will be a boy called Paul – growing up here in this place that he hates so much. Vivian suggests the name Molly; they joke about having twins, Paul and Paulette; they lie there in the field, embracing.

Chapter Fifteen

Vivian meets Tante Lou.

As they get ready to return, they talk about the Christmas programs (nativity plays, songs) they have to organize for their schools. Grant has not yet begun, as the *"stuff in Bayonne"* (p. 106, l. 14) has been keeping him too busy to think about other things.

When they return to the quarter, people are leaving the church. Vivian asks if she should leave before his aunt returns, but Grant wants her to stay and meet his aunt, as he has told her he has a girlfriend in Bayonne.

Vivian's own love history has not been not happy: coming from a small rural community, Free LaCove, she had met and married a very dark-skinned young man in secret while studying. Her family was furious and refused to talk to him. When she went back to show her family her first child, no one had acknowledged it. That had been

Even among blacks there is prejudice concerning dark skin.

three years ago, and she had not gone back home since, not even when her second child was born or when she had separated from her husband.

His aunt and her friends arrive at the house, where Grant and Vivian await them. She refuses to look at Grant but greets Vivian, albeit with the minimum of politeness. Following her lead, the other women refrain from being overly polite or friendly to Vivian.

They gather in the kitchen. Grant offers to make coffee, but his aunt insists that she can do it herself. Grant describes Vivian as the woman he is going to marry. Grant can see exactly how his aunt tries to handle this new situation: she could physically force her way around him to make the coffee, which might provoke him to leave; she could leave herself, which would mean her friends would then have to leave with her after having just seated themselves; or she could sit down and let Grant make the coffee, which course of action would have no victim but her own pride. She takes a seat.

Tante Lou focuses her attention on Vivian. She asks about Free LaCove, Vivian's home town, as she has heard that the people there don't like dark-skinned people. Vivian agrees that that is true for some of the people there. Still being blunt and unfriendly, Grant's aunt asks about her own relatives: Vivian admits that she doesn't go back. Tante Lou wants to know if she doesn't love her own parents. Vivian says she does – but she has to live her own life.

The interrogation moves on to religion – does Vivian attend church? She does. She is Catholic. Was she in church on this Sunday? Last Sunday? Will she attend service next Sunday? The Sunday after? And, Tante Lou points out, Grant has no religion – what will Vivian do about that? Vivian remains calm and responds to Tante Lou's brusque questioning. She firmly replies that she and Grant will work things out.

Afterwards, Vivian and Grant go out to the porch. He indirectly apologizes for his aunt's behavior, and Vivian says that she can see that her parents are not "*the only ones*" (p. 111, l. 12). Grant dismisses this immediately, saying it is "*far from being the same thing*" (p. 111, l. 13), which seems to upset or offend Vivian. She says she must go, and goes back into the house to get her things and say goodbye. Grant hears his aunt telling her she has "*quality*" (p. 111, l. 24), and urging her not to give up on God. The other women join in now saying that she is pretty, has good manners, and is obviously a lady of quality. She leaves Grant with a playful comment about how, being a lady of such quality, she could not possibly kiss him in public.

Chapter Sixteen

Miss Emma's visit to Jefferson

This chapter contains a flashback sequence embedded within another scene, and this flashback is itself a third-hand account of events. Other chapters in the novel cover more than one time frame, but this chapter is, in this respect, the most complicated.

Grant is walking around the schoolhouse when he sees Miss Emma and Reverend Ambrose return from their visit to Jefferson. Grant has been arranging the school Christmas program and getting a Christmas tree.

Before dismissing the class, Grant asks them all "*to remember one person during this Christmas season. I'm sure I don't have to remind you who I'm thinking about.*" (p. 114, ll. 7–9).

After the class has left, Grant is sitting in the schoolroom, correcting a geography test his pupils have done. One of his pupils reappears saying that Miss Emma has asked Grant to stop by on his way home.

When he arrives at Emma's house, his aunt and Reverend Ambrose are both there as well. He senses immediately that the visit to Grant has gone badly. Miss Emma tells Grant that she knows he lied to her after his last visit to Jefferson, that Jefferson hadn't enjoyed the food she made for him, and that he hadn't asked how she was.

A couple of days later – the narration jumps forward in time in the middle of this scene in the kitchen – Grant finally learns what happened. Miss Eloise Bouie calls on his aunt, and he overhears her telling her friend what happened in the jail cell. Jefferson ignored them when they were there and, when he finally looked at Miss Emma, his expression was "*blank*". The Reverend Ambrose began talking about God, and Jefferson looked at the preacher with hatred, as if he wanted to say something "*cruel, mean*".

Miss Emma tried to interest Jefferson in the food, but he asked in an expressionless way for corn, "*Corn for a hog*" (p. 116, l. 20). He didn't ask to be born, he said. He continued like this until Emma slapped him. She then collapsed in tears over his unresponsive body, and remained there until the deputy came.

Back in the present, Miss Emma breaks down in tears again, wondering what she had done to make the Lord punish her like this. Reverend Ambrose tells her that the Lord doesn't hate her, that he is just testing her. Emma doesn't respond but instead she looks straight at Grant and tells him to return. He can't understand what they expect him to achieve. He tells them that Jefferson behaved in exactly the same way with him when he was there, that the young man wanted to make him feel guilty, which he didn't, and that Grant spends his time trying to make sure that other young men didn't end up where Jefferson now was. His aunt orders him to return.

Chapter Seventeen

A conversation with Jefferson

This chapter covers the week between Miss Emma's visit to Jefferson on the Monday, and Grant's next visit on the Friday. It contains three important encounters – with the sympathetic white deputy Paul Bonin, a first real conversation with Jefferson, and another confrontation with Sheriff Guidry.

Grant goes to the courthouse on Friday and strikes up a conversation with the young deputy, Paul Bonin, who he decides is the most likely of the officers to be honest with him. The two of them, Grant and Paul, are close in age, and he can tell that Paul is better educated than Sheriff Guidry or the other deputy. In addition, Grant has learned from people in the black quarter that Bonin's family are decent people. Grant asks Paul about Jefferson, and Paul tells him what he knows. Paul asks Grant to use his first name with him, and then they shake hands. He tells Grant that he has been warned not to get too close to prisoners who have been sentenced to death and that he will be decent and "*treat him right*" (p. 120, l. 16), but not get involved. Grant says that he feels the same way.

Jefferson is sitting despondently on his bunk, staring out of the window. Grant greets him and offers him food, but Jefferson says he is not hungry. Grant tells him that they must talk. He tells Jefferson that Miss Emma had broken down after her visit to him. Grant asks him if that is what he wants – for her to return home in tears after each visit. Jefferson says nothing. Grant insists that he can make it easier for his godmother – that all she wants is for somebody to do something for her before she dies. Jefferson points out that it is he who will be dying. Grant asks if it is too much to ask that Jefferson show some concern for others. Jefferson asks, "*Cause I'm go'n die anyway – that's what you trying to say?*" (p. 122, l. 14). He tells Jefferson that we all die – but Jefferson counters with the question of when. Grant says he doesn't know when – and that is why he tries to live as well as he can, and not hurt others, especially not others people who love him and have made sacrifices for him. He wants to help those people as much as he can. Jefferson says that Grant can talk like that because he is not imprisoned in one of the cells, facing death. Grant asks him where the benefit is in hurting people who love him. Jefferson accuses Grant of bothering him.

The conversation turns ugly at this point. Jefferson starts making insinuations about Vivian – he says he will say something about *"that old yellow woman"* (p. 123, l. 2) (Vivian is much lighter-skinned than Jefferson or Grant) if Grant continues to annoy him. Grant tells him that it is Vivian that keeps him coming to visit Jefferson. Jefferson then threatens to scream. Grant asks Jefferson if he really wants Sheriff Guidry to come and throw Grant out, which would be the consequence. Jefferson does not scream. He sees that Jefferson needs and wants him to stay – if only so that he can insult him.

Here for the first time Jefferson shows strong emotions. Jefferson's despair expresses itself as hostility or apathy.

Jefferson then makes an obscene comment about Vivian which almost drives Grant to violence. But he sees that Jefferson's grinning face is actually an expression of deep pain. Grant tells Jefferson that he is only coming because of Vivian – not because of his aunt or Jefferson's godmother. Jefferson is moved to tears but replies coldly that good manners are for the living. He knocks the bag of food onto the floor and says that food is for the living, too.

On his way out, Grant learns that Sheriff Guidry has asked to see him. When he gets to the Sheriff's office, Grant sees that the older deputy is there, as well as the fat man he had seen at Pichot's house. Guidry complains that Miss Emma, Tante Lou and Reverend Ambrose have demanded a more comfortable place to meet in, as there is not enough room in the cell to sit down. Guidry believes that Grant has something to do with this, which Grant denies.

He later learns that Miss Emma, his aunt and the Reverend had visited the sheriff's wife, Edna Guidry, after their visit to Jefferson. Edna Guidry had shown unusual hospitality (for a white woman of high social standing) by having black people served coffee in the living room. Miss Emma then reminded her of the many years she had served the Guidry family and urged Mrs Guidry to speak to her husband about organizing more comfortable conditions for her visits to Jefferson. Edna Guidry feels uncomfortable and says that she'll be *"glad when all this is over"* (p. 126, ll. 32–3) (from her perspective, the whole complicated business: but for Miss Emma this, of course, means simply the execution of her godson), provoking a display of grief on Miss Emma's part. The pressure Miss Emma exerted on Edna Guidry pays off, as she spoke to her husband about the matter.

Note how previously the black characters were only allowed into the kitchen.

Sheriff Guidry asks Jefferson how he feels about it. He will be given the choice between meeting in the dayroom, in handcuffs and leg chains, or continuing to receive visitors in his cell without being shackled.

Chapter Eighteen

Another difficult visit to Jefferson

Jefferson doesn't say either no or yes to the dayroom visits, so Guidry gives his permission, and the next visit by Miss Emma and Reverend Ambrose takes place in the dayroom. Miss Emma lays out the food she has brought like a picnic. Jefferson is led in, shackled, and told that he is not allowed to move from his chair for the duration of the visit. Jefferson is unresponsive. He won't talk to his godmother or eat. She is deeply hurt.

Note that food always plays an important role in the visits to the jail – it is a symbol of Miss Emma's love.

When Grant next comes, he also meets Jefferson in the dayroom. He has brought food from Miss Emma. At first Jefferson is not responsive. When he says he wants to talk about *"that chair"* (p. 131, l. 5), Grant starts talking about the preparations for the Christmas program at school, as he does not want to discuss his death.

Grant asks if Jefferson knows what "*moral*" or "*obligation*" mean. Grant explains that, no matter how badly off people are, they still owe something: Jefferson owes, too. Not to Grant, and not to Sheriff Guidry, but to his godmother. He must show her understanding and love. Jefferson says again that such things are for humans. He isn't human. He can't give love as he is just a hog.

Grant asks if he prefers meeting here in the dayroom, or up in his cell – predictably, Jefferson claims not to care. Grant says he should care for Miss Emma's sake – each time she returns from having visited him at the courthouse, she looks worse. Jefferson says she should stay at home. Grant tells him that would just make her worry more. "*Hogs don't worry,*" Jefferson says, "*hogs just know.*" (p. 132, l. 18) Grant points out that hogs know nothing. Jefferson knows: "*This hog know. Fattening up for Christmas. Kill him at Christmastime.*" The "*old hog*" (p. 132, ll. 21–2), he says, will be glad when this is all over.

Grant then goes to meet Vivian. He picks her up as she is finishing work and they go to the Rainbow Club. They had agreed to go to Baton Rouge that weekend to have some time together, but Grant now doesn't want to. They have discovered that their sex life suffers after Grant's visits to Jefferson. He tells her that he would drop everything and leave with her now if she gave the word. She says that if they did, they would hate each other for the rest of their lives: Grant refuses to believe he could ever hate her. He protests that nothing he is doing at the courthouse is doing any good, that nothing is changing. She replies that something is changing.

Chapter Nineteen

The Christmas program at the school

This chapter describes the wintry weather in the fortnight preceding the Christmas program staged at the school, and the program itself. Grant has told his students that this year's program is dedicated to Jefferson, so many more people come to see it than had been expected.

At seven o'clock Grant opens the program, greeting the audience. He asks Reverend Ambrose to lead them in a prayer. Ambrose recites the Lord's Prayer, and then goes on to thank God for the gift of a new day, and asks Him to look after the sick and afflicted, and all those in jail cells across the country, and all those who either knew Him not or felt they had no need of Him. No matter how educated a man might be (Grant knows here that Ambrose means him), the Reverend says, without faith he is locked in a cold, dark cell of ignorance.

The program begins, with songs and a Christmas tree under which lies a package – a present for Jefferson. There are further songs and readings before a nativity play is performed. This ends the program. Reverend Ambrose closes the program with another prayer, largely repeating what he said before.

The program is a success, but Grant is unhappy. What has upset him is the fact that everything is always the same – the program is the same, the songs are the same, the minister's prayers are the same, the clothes the audience wear is the same – and the following year it will be the same again. He does not feel that anything is changing.

Again, we get the feeling that no change is possible, and that Antoine's cynicism and Jefferson's despair are justified.

Chapter Twenty

The date of Jefferson's execution

Towards the end of February, Grant is summoned to Henri Pichot's house together with Reverend Ambrose so that they can break the news to Miss Emma about the date of the execution.

Guidry tells them that the execution has been set for the second Friday after Easter. Grant asks why they chose that particular date. Guidry says that it had to be before or after Easter, and it couldn't have been during Lent.

Grant later learns from Paul Bonin that the execution had originally been scheduled for two weeks before Ash Wednesday, but that another execution was already scheduled for that date, and the substantial Catholic population in the area would have taken offence at two executions being conducted right before Lent.

Grant is still allowed to visit Jefferson in jail, but he now knows he has just over a month: the execution has been set for Friday April 8th, between one and three in the afternoon.

Grant is stunned by the events. He cannot grasp how a date and time can be set so casually for the death of a man. He marvels at this "*justice*" – "*Twelve white men say a black man must die, and another white man sets the date and time without consulting one black person.*" (p. 150, ll. 12–14). Grant ponders the injustice – that for simply having been in the wrong place at the wrong time, Jefferson has been imprisoned and will be killed at white people's convenience.

Here is an example of Ambrose's strength, which Grant refuses to aknowledge.

The two men are dismissed: Ambrose offers to give Grant a ride down to the quarter, but Grant refuses to be the one to break the news to Miss

Emma. Ambrose tells him he would have the strength if he had God.

Chapter Twenty-One

Grant goes to Miss Emma's house, and Vivian visits him at home

This chapter is especially important for its look at the roles of men and women in the black community.

Grant goes to Miss Emma's house. It is crowded with people. Emma herself is in bed, stunned by the news. Tante Lou and Reverend Ambrose both give Grant harsh looks. Grant no longer cares what Reverend Ambrose thinks of him.

Soon after he has returned home, Vivian arrives. He makes her a coffee and they sit in his room. He is very glad that she has come to see him. They talk about whether she should go to Miss Emma's house to pay her respects; Grant thinks that she should. They leave for Emma's house.

Vivian is taken to see Miss Emma, who is pleased to hear what she says. They then go to the kitchen, where Grant's aunt ignores Grant and once again treats Vivian with a kind of politeness that masks her distrust and her possessive feelings concerning her nephew. Irene Cole is also introduced to Vivian, and is also polite but cold to her.

Miss Emma tells Grant that she doesn't know when she will be able to return to the courthouse – that it all rests now with him and Reverend Ambrose. She hopes they will work together. He promises to try.

He and Vivian then leave for the Rainbow Club, where Vivian tells Grant she thinks that Irene Cole is in love with him, due to the coldness with which she treated her. Grant is also aware of this, and says that it is the same with his aunt; her love for him is jealous, and both she and Irene dislike the fact that an "*outsider*" is stealing him away. But they are talking on different levels; Grant is talking generally, seeing himself as a young man whom people want to hold on to because they have so little of anything else: but Vivian is talking quite specifically about Irene Cole's feelings of love.

Grant explains that what Irene and his aunt want from him is the same thing that Miss Emma wants from Jefferson – somebody to be proud of. Emma knows that the state of Louisiana is about to take his life, and she wants something to remember him by. The same is true for Irene and Tante Lou – both know that Grant will leave. And they both want to fight against that. He says that what Miss Emma wants is memories of Jefferson – not just to know that his soul has been saved.

Here Grant explains the expectations of black women and the failure of black men to live up to these expectations.

He explains that black men have failed to protect their women since the days of slavery. They either stay and are broken, or run away, leaving the women alone with the children. The women hope with the birth of every male child that this one will somehow break this cycle; but the burden is too great and he must always fail, either by staying to be broken or by fleeing to save himself.

What Miss Emma wants, he says, is for Jefferson and him to "*change everything that has been going on for three hundred years*" (p. 159, ll. 13–14). She wants to be able to say that, before he died, he was a man, proud and upright; that he didn't crawl before the white man. It will be her last chance to see a black man stand up straight for her.

For Tante Lou and Irene it is the same. His aunt has had nothing – she never married. She raised Grant's mother because her sister, Grant's grandmother, moved somewhere else, just like Grant's parents themselves later moved to California, leaving Grant with her. She and Irene and all the other women in the quarter look around and see only broken men. Grant, on the other hand, went away, got educated, and returned, and now they want to hold on to him as tightly as they can – not realizing that this will also break him. To remain himself – the Grant that they love and admire and in whom they place their hopes – Grant must also leave.

Jefferson must learn to stand up and show he has not been broken by the system.

Vivian asks him if this vicious cycle can be broken; he tells her that it is up to Jefferson now.

Chapter Twenty-Two

The radio

Grant arrives at the courthouse, where Jefferson has been informed of the date of his execution.

This is the first time Jefferson opens up.

Jefferson asks Grant what day it is – it's a Friday. He seems to be more communicative than he has been before Grant asks him if he wants anything, and Jefferson says he wants a gallon of ice cream – he smiles, and for the first time the smile is not bitter. He says that he has never had enough ice cream, that he wants a whole gallon, and he wants to eat it with a large spoon. When Grant tells him some news from the quarter, he appears calmer than before, and is even momentarily interested in the birth of a child, before he realizes that on the day of the shooting,

Note the contrast between Jefferson's desire for a gallon of ice cream and his refusal to eat his aunt's food.

he was supposed to have gone hunting with the father of the child. Grant continues to talk about the quarter, and then suggests that he could bring Jefferson a radio, so that he could listen to music in his cell. Jefferson would like a radio, but his interest is flagging, and he becomes inert and depressed again.

As usual when this happens, Grant is unable to leave, for fear that the sheriff would then misinterpret the reason and cancel his visits, so he waits until the hour is up. When Paul comes to collect him, he tells him about the radio, which Paul thinks is a good idea.

Grant will have to borrow the money to buy the radio. He goes to the Rainbow Club to wait until Vivian has finished work so that he can ask her for the money. He tells Clairborne, the barman, who collects a couple of dollars from the other bar patrons and gives Grant $5 of his own money. Grant goes round to the other side of the Club to get something to eat. Thelma Clairborne gives him the rest of the money he needs for the radio, saying that he shouldn't ask Vivian for the money as she has children to support.

Grant sets off to buy a radio. He is treated with contempt by the white shop assistant: he has to insist on being given a new radio, rather than the display piece, and is left waiting while the shop assistant goes to serve a white customer.

He returns to the courthouse, where Sheriff Guidry has been informed about the radio; the Sheriff is not happy about the radio, but permits it. He tells Grant that, in future, all such requests are to be made to him, and not to the junior deputy.

Chapter Twenty-Three

The radio becomes controversial.
Jefferson loves his radio and listens to it all the time. When Miss Emma, who is feeling better, accompanies Reverend Ambrose to see him in the dayroom, he refuses to leave his cell if he can't take the radio with him, so she packs up all the food and goes to the cell. When Paul returns to the cell, as he later tells Grant, the radio is off and Jefferson is lying on his bunk with his back to his visitors. Sheriff Guidry then wants to know from Miss Emma if Jefferson was giving her any trouble. He is suspicious about the radio, and about Jefferson's refusal to come to the dayroom. He doubts Miss Emma's claims to be content to visit with Jefferson in his cell, after she had pressured Edna Guidry to request the use of the dayroom from the sheriff.

That day, after school is finished, Grant is summoned to Miss Emma's house. He arrives there to find her, Reverend Ambrose, and his aunt gathered. His aunt and the Reverend are both angry with Grant for having given Jefferson the radio. They say that all he does is listen to it all day long. Grant doesn't see a problem with that. He insists that Jefferson needs something with him in the cell – Ambrose agrees, but says that what he needs with him is God, not "*that sin box*" (p. 172, l. 30). The Reverend considers the music Jefferson listens to be sinful – Grant calls it company. The two argue again.

Grant tells them that the last time he visited Jefferson he had looked at him for the first time without hate or accusation. He tells them that he has found a way to reach Jefferson by give him something that he wants – the radio, and the promise of ice cream. He says that he wants to make Jefferson's last month as comfortable as he can. His aunt is contemptuous of this, as she is worried about his soul. Grant points out that she sent him to see Jefferson, and that he is doing the best he can and that the radio helps him not think about death. He threatens to not go to the courthouse again if they take Jefferson's radio away from him.

Reverend Ambrose is angry with Grant for insisting on having it his way. Grant insists that the only thing which stops Jefferson from thinking that he is a hog is the radio. The Reverend says that he then is the one who is not needed. Emma however still wants Ambrose to go to Jefferson. Ambrose says that Jefferson can't hear him "*through that wall of sin*" (p. 174, l. 20). Miss Emma is certain that Jefferson will need Reverend Ambrose, even if neither he nor Grant knows it yet.

That week, Grant gets the children at the school to collect pecans and roasted peanuts for him to take to Jefferson. He takes these, along with some fruit, candy, and comic books.

In the jail cell, he talks with Jefferson, and tells him how upset Miss Emma was about not being able to meet him in the dayroom. Grant extracts from Jefferson a promise that, on her next visit, he will meet her in the dayroom, and that he will allow Reverend Ambrose to talk with him.

Grant then tells Jefferson that he wants to be his friend. He wants Jefferson to be able to talk to him about anything that comes into his head. He then suggests that he could bring Jefferson a notebook and a pencil to note down his thoughts, so that he could later talk about them. Jefferson

Grant offers to give Jefferson a notebook so he can write down his thoughts.

signals agreement, but has again retreated into his own thoughts.

As Grant is leaving, Jefferson suddenly and with great difficulty asks him to thank the children for the pecans and peanuts. Grant is elated – he has the feeling that he has finally broken through.

Chapter Twenty-Four

A talk with Jefferson

Miss Emma decides that they should visit Jefferson together. On the way to the courthouse Grant stops to buy the notebook and pencil he had promised Jefferson. His aunt and Ambrose both seem to be angry with him, but Miss Emma isn't, and Grant has decided that it is her feelings which count.

Inside the courthouse they are met by the senior deputy. Once in the dayroom, Miss Emma spreads out her tablecloth and lays out the food she has brought. The deputy brings Jefferson. The Reverend Ambrose begins to pray before the meal, asking God to touch the hearts of all there. Neither Grant nor Jefferson responds to the prayer. They then begin eating – except for Jefferson, who says he is not hungry, and Miss Emma. Grant is the only one who seems able to make conversation with Jefferson. He tells him that he brought him the notebook and pencil. Jefferson says that he has thought of some questions for Grant, but then he says nothing.

Grant suggests that he and Jefferson walk around the room for a while. Grant reminds Jefferson that he wants to be his friend. He also tells Jefferson that he wants him to be a friend to his godmother – to be more than a godson. He persuades Jefferson to eat at least a little of the gumbo she has brought for him, to please her.

A talk about heroes

A conversation of major importance in the novel now follows. Grant talks about heroes and the nature of heroism with Jefferson – *"A hero is someone who does something for other people."* (p. 181, ll. 28–9). Using himself as an example of what a hero is not – *"I want to run away. I want to live for myself and my woman and for nobody else"* (p. 182, ll. 1–3) – he explains to Jefferson that he wants him to become a hero. To become the man who will give the quarter something to believe in. He believes that Jefferson can prove the white men wrong – the men who believe, and say, that Jefferson is a hog and not a man. He wants Jefferson to embody the dignity and love of the community.

Grant urges Jefferson to destroy the myth that white men are superior.

Grant moves on to myths. *"A myth is an old lie that people believe in."* (p. 182, ll. 27–8). White people, he says, believe the myth that they are better than everyone else. They don't want to see a black man standing up straight, with pride and dignity. Grant says that as long as black men do not stand up strong to illustrate the wrongs of slavery (and the segregation that followed it), then white men will be safe with their myth. He wants Jefferson to stand up and prove them liars by doing so.

He tells Jefferson that he, Grant, needs him more than Jefferson could ever need him. He says that he must stay here where he is needed, teaching, even though it is choking him. He asks Jefferson to tell him what to do. He insists that Jefferson can be greater than anyone else he has ever met. Grant says that Jefferson must change himself to become something better, both for himself and for them all.

Grant believes that Jefferson is crying because he feels that he still belongs.

Chapter Twenty-Five

Grant gets in a fight at the Rainbow Club

After the visit to the courthouse, Grant goes to the Rainbow Club while the others return to the quarter. He wants to see Vivian and tell her about the day with Jefferson. He thinks of Reverend Ambrose's envy of his success in reaching Jefferson and how the minister wished to have control of Jefferson's last days, fearing that it would be sin and the sinner (Grant) who would succeed in granting Miss Emma's wish to see her godson die a man.

Here, we see Grant's uncharitable side; it seems as though making Reverend Ambrose envious is as important as getting through to Jefferson.

The bar at the Rainbow is empty except for a few old men and a couple of mulatto bricklayers. The mulattoes in the area work mostly in construction, in order to avoid having to work with the blacks in the fields. They even manage to get work which would normally be done by whites, because they work for less money. Grant knows that the mulattoes also tend to drop out of school early to learn a trade rather than spend time sitting with the blacks in school. Ignorant and prejudiced, the mulattoes don't dare go to the white bars in the town.

Grant sits and drinks and half-listens to the mulattoes' conversation, who are talking in an insulting manner about Jefferson, saying that he should have been killed long ago. He knows that they are talking intentionally loudly enough for him to hear them, but he tries to remain calm. Finally he goes over to the mulattoes and tells them to shut up. A fight breaks out. The Clairbornes try to break up the brawl, and

The violence here reminds the reader of the violence that has resulted in many young black men being killed or put in jail.

eventually Grant is knocked unconscious by Joe Clairborne. Vivian arrives to take Grant away.

Chapter Twenty-Six

Grant and Vivian argue.

Vivian takes Grant back to her home and looks after his injuries from the fight. She is furious with him for having got involved in a fight. They both know that she may now be in trouble for another reason: having a young man in her home when her husband is away in Houston. Grant says he will leave, but he has been hurt on the head. Grant tries to excuse his behavior but she says that it is in this way that "*you all*" (young black men) get killed.

Grant tries to tell her about his success with Jefferson that day. Vivian, however, is preoccupied and tells him that her husband will only give her a divorce if he can see the children regularly. They both assume that the husband does this in order to make it impossible for Vivian and Grant – he apparently knows they have a relationship – to leave the area. They then argue about what their love is based on, as she feels he concentrates too much on love-making without considering for her problems and feelings.

Chapter Twenty-Seven

Grant and Reverend Ambrose talk

On a Sunday after church, the Reverend Ambrose comes to visit and talk about Jefferson. The Reverend is worried that Jefferson is not yet saved, i.e. will not go to heaven. Grant doesn't see this as being his responsibility, but Ambrose says it is, as Jefferson listens to him. Ambrose asks

Grant if he ever thinks of anybody but himself. Grant sees his work as being in the field of *"reading, writing and arithmetic"*, and the Reverend's in the saving of souls.

Ambrose says that he is going to talk to Jefferson about God on his next visit. He says that he needs Grant's help in preparing Jefferson for the afterlife, but Grant doesn't believe in this other world. Grant says he does believe in God. He reminds Ambrose that Miss Emma merely asked him to help Jefferson walk to his death like a man.

Reverend Ambrose attacks Grant's notions of education. He says that reading, writing and arithmetic are not enough – that Grant is ignorant. He warns Grant that he won't let him *"send that boy's soul to hell"* (p. 204, l. 12). Grant says he's welcome to Jefferson if he wants him; they don't have to fight for him.

Ambrose demands that Grant tell Jefferson to fall on his knees before his godmother on the way to the chair. Grant refuses do this. Ambrose, furious and disgusted, tells Grant that he is *"lost"*. Grant will not stand in the way of Jefferson's faith, but he will not lie to him about heaven or the soul, things in which he either doesn't believe or about which he knows nothing. He says he will never lie to Jefferson again.

Reverend Ambrose tells Grant that he has to lie all the time. He knows that this is why Grant looks down on him – but this is his idea of the purpose of education, to alleviate pain, if necessary by lying. He tells Grant that that is how Tante Lou lives – lying to herself about her own suffering so as not to trouble Grant with it, allowing him to study and become educated. The Reverend's point here is very similar to the argument Grant himself

In this section we are shown how lying is one way of helping other people. If it is done with love, it can be a form of strength.

had made about the need for a strong young black man. Ambrose knows his people, he knows their pain, and knows that all their suffering and sacrifice is endured in the hope that someone they love will one day come back and take away their pain.

The idea of sacrifice is important in the novel.

Chapter Twenty-Eight

The last visit: Grant and Jefferson talk about faith and death.

In Jefferson's cell, the two men talk about God, heaven, faith and death. Grant is unable to answer Jefferson's questions, but Jefferson is finding his own answers now, and Grant feels humbled by the dignity and wisdom now budding in Jefferson.

This is the last account of a visit by Grant to Jefferson before his execution.

Chapter Twenty-Nine

Jefferson's notebook

This chapter contains the entries and fragments Jefferson wrote in the notebook Grant gave him, all of them addressed to Grant. All the thoughts, feelings and doubts which have been inside him, and which he could not or would not express, can be found here. There are 40 entries in the notebook. They show Jefferson's awareness of the world around him, the view from his cell window and the sounds of the other prisoners; they reveal his fears of death and his confusion and doubt about the message of God that Ambrose brings him, about his belief that God only loves white people, about his struggle to understand the nature of love. He describes a visit to his cell from Henri Pichot, Sheriff Guidry and Dr. Morgan, and the attention he receives from Clark (the senior deputy) and Paul. He writes that he knows them, all of them, even if he has never before given an indication of understanding who and what they are. Children come to visit him in his cell, as do other people from the quarter, and Jefferson is both moved and disturbed by the attention and love shown him. He writes that he has told Miss Emma that he is now strong, as strong as she wanted him to become. As the date approaches, he thanks Grant for having been the first person to make him feel like somebody.

On the last night, Sheriff Guidry visits him. He wants to make sure that Jefferson is also writing in his notebook about how fairly the Sheriff and his deputies had treated him, allowing him visitors and being decent to him. Jefferson assures him that he will include this, too. Guidry, as he appears in Jefferson's notebook, seems to be feeling in a way guilty.

The last few entries are fragments, scrawled during his last night on earth. His terror and regret are painfully evident. His last impressions are of dawn; the sycamore tree and birds outside his window; the blue sky; and of his own strength and the fact that he is a man.

Chapter Thirty

The day of the execution

The executioner, Henry Vincent, arrives, and the electric chair is prepared. This chapter is not written from Grant's perspective, but instead offers a panorama of perspectives from around the town, both white and black. It describes the passing of the last night and the preparations for the funeral in an initially cool and distanced, yet increasingly disturbed and fraught manner.

The chapter ends with Jefferson asking Paul to accompany him on his last walk.

Chapter Thirty-One

The end

Grant is at school, but cannot work. No one from the black quarter is working on the afternoon of the execution. He is thinking about his childhood, about other children. He thinks that, after today, nothing will ever be the same again.

Oppressed by the impending execution, Grant again feels the urge to flee, to get into his car and drive far away from Bayonne. He needs to be with Vivian, and worries about Jefferson – he knows that Reverend Ambrose is with him, and he now acknowledges the strength of the old minister. Alone, Grant asks himself why he lacks the courage or strength to be with Jefferson – or even to be with his own pupils, whom he has ordered to stay on their knees for the duration within the church. He is tortured with anxieties about where Jefferson now is, what he is doing and feeling on his way to his own execution. His awareness of the gross injustice done to Jefferson – standing for the entire black experience in this time and place – is intense and painful. He refuses to place his faith in a white man's God and a white man's judicial system, both of which disenfranchise the blacks. He refuses to believe himself, yet he knows that the rest of the quarter must believe, that belief in something is the only way they can achieve their freedom. As he sits and waits under a pecan tree, he sees a yellow butterfly land near him and then fly away. He knows that it is all over now; that Jefferson is dead.

Being an educated man does not mean that one is also a strong person.

As he walks back into the quarter a car approaches. Paul Bonin has come to see Grant, and to give him Jefferson's notebook. The two men walk together, and Paul tells him about the execution. He says that at the end, Jefferson had been the strongest man present. His last words were "*Tell Nannan I walked*" (p.240, l.13). Paul tells Grant that he is a great teacher, but Grant says he isn't, that one has to believe to be able to teach. But Paul insists, saying that he saw the transformation – what became of Jefferson during his time in jail. Grant does not want to accept responsibility for this, but Paul doesn't believe it was Jefferson's work alone, and Grant can't believe it was God.

Paul asks if he could read what Jefferson wrote some time. He compliments Grant on Vivian. They arrive at Miss Emma's house; Paul is leaving and Grant is going to go in. They part as friends, clasping hands, Paul saying that he will never forget this day, or Jefferson.

Background Information

Racial Segregation in the USA

The segregation of blacks and whites in America has a long history going back to slavery. Even following the Civil War and the Reconstruction era, blacks remained in every respect "second class citizens" up until the Civil Rights Movement of the 1960s. During the time in which the novel is set, racial segregation in Louisiana was in full effect: for example, throughout the 1940s, less than 1% of all blacks in the state were able to vote.

One distinction made in the study of racial segregation is between *de jure* (legally required separation of races) and *de facto* segregation, which arose from cultural, traditional, or economic developments and were not enforced by law. Whereas *de jure* segregation (the so-called "separate but equal" laws accepted by the US Supreme Court) had been modified and in some cases weakened by legislation before its final abolishment in the 1960s, the *de facto* forms had a most damaging impact on the black community and continue today. This form of discrimination and active separatism has proved more difficult to fight, as it is built on cultural prejudices. The concrete results of *de jure* segregation meant that entire urban and rural areas became "*black*" or "*white*". Even after the segregation laws were abolished, many of these areas, however, remained segregated. Schools and other facilities in "*black*" areas remained "*black*". Some areas in towns and cities became ghettoes as a result of this separation.

Segregation	"Separate but equal"
Segregation is the "*act or policy of separating people of different races, religions or sexes and treating them in a different way*" (Oxford Advanced Learner's Dictionary).	*Separate but equal* became a standard phrase encapsulating the essence of American racial segregation in the 19th century. It was intended to illustrate that "*coloreds*" would be treated

Segregation by law (*de jure* segregation) occurred when laws (local, state, or national) required or explicitly allowed racial separation. *De facto* segregation occurs when acts or circumstances, whether social, political, or economic, result in the separation of people by race or ethnicity even though no laws require or authorize racial separation. *De facto* segregation has continued even when state and federal civil rights laws have explicitly prohibited racial segregation.	separately, but equally. After the end of the Civil War, the Morrill Act of 1880 established the legal concept of *separate but equal*, embodying the institutionalization of segregation: *Provided, That no money shall be paid out under this act to any State or Territory for the support and maintenance of a college where a distinction of race or color is made in the admission of students, but the establishment and maintenance of such colleges separately for white and colored students shall be held to be a compliance with the provisions of this act if the funds received in such State or Territory be equitably divided as hereinafter set forth.*

De jure segregation arose following the Civil War. Prior to this, the institution of slavery had made legislation for blacks irrelevant. Immediately after the Civil War, so-called Black Codes were introduced, enforcing segregation.

After the End of Slavery

The Reconstruction era (1865–1877) saw Republican politicians attempt to break these laws. Most of the Black Codes had been dismissed by 1868, and in 1875 the Republican-dominated Congress passed laws prohibiting racial segregation in public facilities and accommodation, i.e. theaters, hotels and restaurants.

This period of progressive and enlightened legislation was abruptly reversed after 1877, when the Union forces finally left the South. Whites used intimidation to prevent blacks from voting, so state legislatures were run by whites, who immediately began introducing the so-called Jim Crow laws. The two major goals of these laws were disenfranchisement and segregation. The disenfranchisement of blacks was enforced by laws restricting who could vote; this affected most blacks as well as many whites. Segregation was enforced in all areas of life – from birth in hospitals, through education in segregated schools, via strict laws on what work blacks were allowed to perform and what property they were allowed to own, to death in segregated cemeteries. There was no area left in which blacks and whites could mingle. Every school, restaurant, hotel, train car, waiting room, elevator, public bathroom, college, hospital, cemetery, swimming pool, drinking fountain, prison, and church was either for whites or blacks but never for both. By making it illegal for blacks to own or rent property in urban areas, cultural *"backwardness"* was enforced as the black population remained poor and rural.

Disenfranchisement

To disenfranchise somebody means to take away their rights, especially their right to vote. In the American South in the years before the Civil Rights Movement of the 1960s, the black population in the South was disenfranchised by legislation such as the introduction of poll taxes and literacy standards, making it almost impossible for poor, uneducated blacks (it had been illegal to teach slaves to read and write, and therefore almost all adult blacks men were illiterate at this time) to be able to exercise their constitutional right to vote. A further method of disenfranchising blacks in the South was the widespread use of mob violence, aggression, intimidation, and even murder (assassinations and lynchings) to terrify the black population into not voting. This era and method is most famously associated with the white supremacist Ku Klux Klan organisation. To provide an example of the effects of the various methods of disenfranchisement: in Louisiana, the setting for *A Lesson Before Dying*, 130,344 blacks registered to vote in 1896. By 1900 that number had been reduced to 5,320.

Changes in the 20th Century

During the 1930s the nature of American politics changed. Whereas up until then the Democrats had, broadly speaking, been the party of the white, land-owning Southern classes, and the Republicans had been associated – especially among blacks – with Abraham Lincoln and abolition, the First World War and the Great Depression led to a shift in the Democratic Party towards a more liberal, urban clientèle in the north. Democratic President Franklin D Roosevelt was strongly opposed to segregation, becoming the first president to appoint African-Americans to political office and appointing the first black federal judge.

The Second World War caused a major change in American perception of race and discrimination. More blacks served in the US Armed Forces than at any time previously, and their services were recognized at home.

A further issue was the nature of Nazi ideology, especially the unprecedented, racially-motivated extremities of the Holocaust. The USA as a whole was becoming sensitized to racism as a threat to freedom and democracy. A further change in the social climate was the understanding that America's racist segregation policies in the South were putting the whole nation in a bad light on the international stage. In the years after the Second World War, many European colonies in Asia and Africa began to win their freedom, creating an international climate opposed to state-sanctioned racism. A further issue was the Cold War, during which Soviet propagandists found an easy target in the brutal and primitive racism of the American South.

The Great Migration

Another change that took place in the first half of the 20th century was a strong, steady movement of blacks out of the rural South and into the northern cities. The reasons for this migration included the search for better jobs, better pay, and a wish to escape the racist oppression of the South. The effects of this migration on the black population were primarily geographic in nature: there were fewer blacks in the South, more in the North, and all across America, the black population was becoming increasingly urbanized. A consequence was that these new concentrations of black populations in cities allowed black voters to unite and elect black representatives to local government, and white politicians with large black constituencies also began to be more active in opposing racial discrimination. Although the North was not entirely free of racism, it did offer a vastly different environment to black people who had been born and raised in the oppressively racist southern states.

The Civil Rights Movement

1968 was the year that saw the end of *de jure* segregation throughout the American South. This was due to the Civil Rights Movement. Between 1955 and 1968 a series of movements started with the aim of ending racial discrimination in America and restoring full voting rights to blacks in the South. Civil disobedience was the primary method used. It combined non-violent protests and direct action (e.g. well-planned activities) to overturn racist legislation and achieve rights for African-Americans. Key events include the court case Brown vs. Board of Education (1954), which began the process of de-segregating schools; the Montgomery bus boycott of 1954–1955, which caused the de-segregation of public transport in 1956; the sit-ins of the 1960s at colleges, libraries, museums and many other public places; and the March on Washington for Jobs and Freedom in 1963, during which Martin Luther King Jr gave his famous *"I have a dream"* speech.

The Movement reached a crisis point in the mid to late 1960s with the assassinations of Martin Luther King, John F Kennedy, and Bobby Kennedy, and race riots in New York, Philadelphia, Los Angeles, Atlanta, Oakland and Detroit. The violence was accompanied by the rise of the Black Power Movement, spearheaded by the Black Panthers, a militant organization led by Huey P. Newton and Bobby Seale.

With the passing of the Civil Rights Act of 1964, which banned discrimination in employment practices and public accommodations, the Voting Rights Act of 1965, which restored voting rights, and the Civil Rights Act of 1968, which banned discrimination in the sale or rental of housing, *de jure* segregation came to an end.

The Historical Context of the Novel

A Lesson Before Dying is set during the 1940s, before the Civil Rights Movement became an important movement. Nevertheless, there is in the character of Grant Wiggins an obvious resistance to accepting the status quo. Higher education was available for African-Americans in separate colleges for blacks but as Grant Wiggins shows there are few blacks from the South who had the basic education and motivation to attend university.

Louisiana, as we see it in the novel, is a strictly segregated society. Blacks and whites live in different areas, work in different capacities, eat and drink and even watch films in different buildings. The *de jure* segregation which regulates life for the black population is further intensified by *de facto* segregation, which permeated the lifestyles, attitudes, behavior, and even the language and communication of both blacks and whites.

The Death Penalty in the USA in the 1940s

The method of execution in Louisiana today is lethal injection. Up until 1938 it was death by hanging; during the time in which *A Lesson Before Dying* is set, it was electrocution.

Capital punishment (the legal term for the death penalty) in the USA was suspended for a brief period in the 1970s, but has a long history before that and has continued since, with 36 states currently using it as a sentence, mostly for specific forms of murder. Arguments for and against the death penalty have been fought for many years now, and the debate is far from finished. One relevant aspect of the debate on the death penalty in America is the demographic make-up of those sentenced to be executed: African-Americans represent 12% of the American population, yet 41% of the inmates of death row. This and other statistics are fiercely debated in discussions on the use of the death penalty in modern societies.

The 1930s had seen more executions in the US than during any other time before or since. During this period, criminologists argued that the death penalty was a necessary preventive measure. This argument is, today, largely irrelevant. Below are some of the most important arguments for and against the death penalty.

Pro	Con
Deterrent The theory that the threat of the death penalty will stop criminals from committing murder or other capital crimes is extremely controversial. Statistics have consistently failed to justify this claim.	**Costs** A 1997 study by the State of Kansas found that death penalty cases are 70% more expensive than life sentences.
Punishment The most basic approach, this is the idea that when a person has broken the laws of the society in which they live, they must suffer unpleasant consequences.	**"Cruel and unusual punishment"** The phrase comes from the 8th Amendment to the US Constitution, forbidding the use of cruel and unusual punishment, and is understood by opponents of the death penalty to include all forms of execution used or once used in the USA – lethal injection, execution, hanging, the gas chamber, and firing squads.
Retribution Drawing its legitimation from the Old Testament ("*an eye for an eye*"; Exodus 21:23–27), this argument understands capital punishment as a moral necessity, serving justice on behalf of the victim.	**Social injustice** Studies have shown that the vast majority of executions in America were of poor, socially-disadvantaged people. This highlights a root issue – that poverty and social discrimination give rise to crime – as well as illuminating a flaw in the justice system; the rich can afford better lawyers, and can also claim to be the more productive and obedient members of society.
Removal Whether the convicted person will remain a threat to others or not, or whether the criminal is incapable of being rehabilitated, this argument claims that the best course of action is to permanently remove the convicted person from society.	

Pro	Con
	Wrong convictions No system is perfect, and one of the most pressing arguments against the death penalty is that there have been proven cases of errors in convicting and sentencing suspects; that people have been executed for crimes for which they were not responsible. **"Killing is wrong"** Amnesty International describes the death penalty as "*the ultimate denial of human rights*". The use of the death penalty as a punishment for killing is illogical, Catholics would argue; a "*tragic illusion that we can teach that killing is wrong by killing*" (Cardinal McCarrick, Archbishop of Washington). This argument is the "*civilized*" response to the Old Testament "*eye for an eye*" philosophy.

The Characters

Grant Wiggins

Grant is the **narrator** and **protagonist** of the novel. He is a young black man, born into a family which had in earlier generations been slaves on the Pichot plantation (p.103 ll.8–10), where he grew up as a child while his aunt worked in the house (p.19, ll.5–25). His parents moved to California during the war (p.99, ll.10–11), and he lives with his aunt, Tante Lou. Grant has been **educated** at university. He left Bayonne ten years before the novel begins to study and returned four years later. Since then he has been working as a **teacher** for the children of the black quarter. He is **having an affair** with a married but separated woman, Vivian, who also works as a teacher, and who lives in Bayonne with her two children.

Grant is asked by his aunt's best friend, Miss Emma Glenn, to help prepare her godson Jefferson for his execution. Grant, the only educated man in the quarter, becomes the focus for the hopes of the black community in his efforts to help the uneducated, under-privileged Jefferson walk to his death like a man.

Grant – the identification figure for the reader – is not an easy character to like or to understand. He is **tormented by inner conflicts**, which make him unable to do anything that will make any difference to anyone – either to himself or to his community. He seems aloof and **self-absorbed** due to his hatred of whites, his frustration with the inertia of the blacks, and his imprisonment in the rigidly unchanging and seemingly unchangeable society in which both communities live.

As an educated black man he is **aware of his own self-worth**, but is treated as an inferior person by the whites. He finds the role he must play to keep the white people happy offensive and demeaning (p.44, ll. 21–26; p. 45, l. 32 – p. 46, l. 5), although he resists it as much as he can without making trouble for himself (pp. 46–49).

His contempt for the black community can be seen in his work as a teacher. He is sarcastic, impatient, vindictive and at times cruel (p. 35, ll. 13–31). This reflects his frustration that nothing will ever change. The description of his former teacher Matthew Antoine (pp. 61–64) indicates that Grant is developing the same hatred towards his students as his teacher had. This same contempt colors his view of the religious faith of the community, which he looks down on as another way of keeping blacks in their place

Besides being torn between his dislike of the whites and his contempt for the blacks, he is also torn between his **desire to escape** from Bayonne (and Louisiana and the South – this is the time of the "*great migrations*" of young black men from the rural South to the northern cities; cf. p. 19, ll. 31–33 and p. 235, ll. 1–2) and his **duty to remain**. This dilemma is one of the central themes of the novel. It is the subject of conversations he has with Vivian, and he also recalls having discussed it with his old teacher, Matthew Antoine (pp. 61–64). Grant is deeply unhappy with his life in Bayonne (p. 28, l. 20 – p. 29, l. 35), describing it as a "*hellhole*" (p. 28, l. 32), yet although he has twice had the chance to get away (once to his parents in California, once when he left for university) he has both times returned. In the end, it is love which keeps him there: his love for those around him, which is stronger than his hatred, and his love for Vivian, for whom he must stay in Bayonne (due to the conditions of the divorce settlement her husband demands).

His frustration makes him at times bitter and hurtful to those around him, and also gives rise to an outburst of violence (pp. 188–190). But this same frustration also makes him eager to spite the white authorities. A recurring example of this is the time he spends in Jefferson's cell; they have been allowed an hour for each visit by Sheriff Guidry, but in the early visits Jefferson lies silent, not responding to Grant. Instead of leaving, Grant always stays for the full hour, knowing that, if he left early, he would be providing Guidry with the excuse he needs to cancel the visits (p. 82, ll. 1–5; p. 132, ll. 31–33).

Grant's initial unwillingness to face the task Miss Emma has set him is worn away by his own growing obsession with Jefferson. His love life suffers (p. 133, ll. 26–29) and he dreams about Jefferson (p. 130, ll. 28–29). The more he has to deal with the young man in prison, the more emotionally involved he becomes. His ideal model of behavior towards a death row inmate (p. 120, ll. 13–18) cannot stand up to the reality of having to confront Jefferson's pain, terror and confusion.

It is the interaction with Jefferson that finally gives Grant a **purpose** to remain and helps him change. At the beginning he is not interested in helping Jefferson: it is yet another pointless chore to him. Slowly, as Jefferson opens up, Grant starts to see Jefferson not merely as another black failure, but as a black man who has been oppressed by white society (*"Twelve white men say a black man must die, and another white man sets the date and time without consulting one black person. Justice?"*, p. 150, ll. 12–14). There are noticeable similarities between the two: their self-absorption at the beginning, the close connection between the two women who are not their mothers and their lack of other family, the violence in their lives (Grant's fight in the Rainbow Club being an example of violence as the primary form of expression, which is why so many young black men end up in prison or dead), the realization that one does things despite oneself (Grant goes to the prison against his own wishes, just as Jefferson learns to do things for the sake of others). Jefferson's ability to face an unjust death as a man serves for Grant as a symbol of hope and redemption for himself, as well as for the black community in Bayonne as a whole. By helping Jefferson find himself in order to be able to approach his death with human dignity, Grant can justify his own presence in this town which he hates so much. Helping Jefferson is also a way of helping himself. He has finally become a teacher and a hero without realizing it. This message is reinforced by Paul Bonin: *"You're one great teacher"* (p. 240, l. 28). One noticeable change that becomes obvious is his attitude to Reverend Ambrose, who is the spiritual leader of the community. While previously he took pleasure in the Reverend's lack of success with Jefferson (p. 185, ll. 26ff.), by the end he acknowledges the strength of character of the Reverend (p. 236, ll. 3–10).

Revision

- Grant Wiggins is the only educated black in the quarter.
- His education cannot help him solve the social problems, which leaves him frustrated and full of resentment.
- He has inner conflicts: between his hatred of the white community and his contempt for the black community; and between his desire to escape and need to remain.
- He loses his contempt for blacks by understanding that he needs Jefferson to show him what it is to be a man.
- There are many parallels between Jefferson and Grant – both are black men who are being crushed by the racist social system.

Key passages	
p. 45, l. 32 – p. 46, l. 5	Grant's ambivalent role in relation to the whites
p. 16, ll. 15–22 pp. 28–29 p. 183, ll. 19–22	His dissatisfaction with his life in Bayonne
p. 92, ll. 22–30 p. 97, ll. 11–27	Grant's loss of faith
pp. 61–64	His conversations with his old teacher, Matthew Antoine
p. 76, l. 22 – p. 75, l. 9	His resentment at the task Miss Emma has set him
p. 30, l. 32 – p. 31, l. 2 p. 117, l. 32 – p. 118, l. 2	His doubts about what Miss Emma has asked him to do
p. 121, l. 31 – p. 124, l. 8	Grant challenges Jefferson's apathetic state for the first time, appealing to his love for his godmother.

pp. 157–160	He explains to Vivian the conditions between men and women in the black communities since the time of slavery. This scene also contains insights into why Grant has been unable to leave Bayonne, despite his hatred of the place
p. 181, l. 13 – p. 184, l. 19	The conversation with Jefferson about heroes and myths is a major scene, illustrating the greater issues behind what Grant and Miss Emma – and, by extension, the whole black community – expect and want from him.

Useful vocabulary: talking about Grant Wiggins

educated • has lost his faith / religious beliefs • self-absorbed • bitter • cynical • makes sarcastic comments • not respected by the white community • looks down on / feels contempt for the black community • feels rage at • humiliates / ridicules his students

Jefferson

Despite being at the center of the story, Jefferson is an **elusive character**. He does not even seem to have a surname. We know that he is young (21 years old; p. 15, l. 15), poor, and uneducated. This elusiveness is an issue for the reader as much as it is for Jefferson himself – lost as he is on the way to his own execution – or for Grant, who is given the task of helping Jefferson find himself.

Inarticulate, ignorant, sullen and uncommunicative, his stupidity and cowardice have led him to be convicted of a murder. At first inspection he is an unrewarding subject for the readers' sympathies as well as for Grant's attentions and efforts. It is not until the last few days before his death that he finds the courage and the need to express himself. Before this we see him as a pathetic, disenfranchised presence (in the court during his trial in the first chapter) that has been robbed of his identity as a man (or human, for that matter). He is for Grant a burden and a chore – ungrateful, unfriendly, unresponsive and apparently so **lost in despair** that it is impossible to help him. Grant feels that Jefferson, in his uglier moments during the earlier visits (p. 80, ll. 1–34), is trying to make those who want to care for him feel guilty (p. 81, ll. 23–25).

Jefferson's self-absorption and lethargy in the face of an injustice that will result in his death makes it very hard for Grant to find a level on which they can communicate. This situation is eventually solved by a combination of various internal and external events and developments. First of all, the radio which Grant brings him in his cell. **This is the first time someone has given Jefferson something that he wants.** Until then, the others were trying to force him to respond according to their needs (the Reverend wanted him to accept God, his godmother wanted him to accept her love, Grant wanted him to communicate). Earlier he had said *"I never got nothing I wanted in my whole life"* (p. 162, ll. 25–26), and had talked about how he wanted a gallon of ice cream on the day he was to die.

However, the radio is merely a spark that helps change Jefferson's attitude. Having been given something he wanted, he is then given peanuts and pecans which have been collected by the children. His offering of thanks (p. 177, l. 14) is the first indication that he is aware of the needs of others. Eventually, the various processes within and around Jefferson – Grant's appeals to Jefferson's intellect (including the request to write in the notebook), emotions, and sense of responsibility to his godmother: his godmother's quiet and unquestioning love; the visits by the various members of the black community; **Jefferson's own journey into himself**, concealed from the reader (and from Grant) until Chapter 29 (pp. 214–222) – enable Jefferson to become less self-absorbed and more aware of what he has to give to his community.

Jefferson embodies in their most extreme forms the issues experienced by Grant and with which the novel is concerned: the racism which makes "justice" a white man's game, and turns "education" into the systematic suppression of opportunities for black children; the violence and threat of death which surrounds young black men; the inability to articulate and express feelings and thoughts which has been cultivated by whites among the black population by *de jure* segregation laws since the days of slavery; the ignorance of self and others; and, finally, the need for **a focal figure of hope for an oppressed community.** So one can view Jefferson as representing the typical black man, held back from achieving his potential due to the inherent injustices of a racist system,

At the same time, the oppressed black community seeks **iconic figures** to look up to, who show that they do deserve respect and that they can achieve something. This can be seen by the reaction of blacks to the achievements in sport by figures such as Jackie Robertson and Joe Louis (pp. 83–87). Their successes made the community feel proud. Framed by the Easter story of the sacrifice of Jesus for the good of humanity, Jefferson's own fate becomes endowed with aspects of heroism and redemption. Yet the strict day-to-day realities of segregation and oppression do not allow for the open acknowledgement of a figure with such power to unite. But by the end of the novel Jefferson has come to embody for the people of the black quarter the essential messages of sacrifice, specifically of the crucifixion and resurrection – that they are saved in and through death, that hope that can be found in despair, that the strength of the weak and oppressed lies in their unity, and that love essentially triumphs.

The connection drawn in the novel between Jefferson and the figure of Jesus is examined more closely on p. 114.

Key passages	
p. 9, l. 5 – p. 10, l. 25	Jefferson as he is understood by the white authorities (even his own defense lawyer)

p. 87, ll. 2–4	Foreshadowing of Jefferson's function as a sacrificial focus for hope and identity
p. 80, ll. 1 – p. 81, l. 16	His self-hatred and despair, expressed in bitter parody of himself as a "*hog*"
pp. 122–124	The first signs of real emotion he shows are during a confrontation with Grant.
p. 162, l. 30 – p. 163, l. 21	Once the date has been set for his execution, Jefferson seems to lose his armor of bitterness and pain. There is genuine delight at the thought of eating ice cream.
p. 174, l. 33 – p. 177	Grant brings Jefferson the sacks of pecans and peanuts which the school children have collected for him. Typically monosyllabic and unresponsive at the beginning of this particular visit, Jefferson at the end shows how deeply touched he is by the gift. His gratitude and the effort is has cost him to show it move Grant deeply and make him realize that he is on the right track.
pp. 207–213 "*I'm the one got to do everything, Mr Wiggins. I'm the one.*" (p. 211, l. 12)	Jefferson has grown into the role for which Grant was to prepare him: his self-pity has given way to unflinching acceptance, and a kind of wisdom is emerging from his confusion and ignorance. This scene evens ends with the unlikely image of Jefferson comforting Grant (p. 213, ll. 4–8)

p. 240, ll. 6–15	An account of how Jefferson died – with dignity.

Useful vocabulary: talking about Grant Wiggins

elusive • self-absorbed • sullen • depressed • withdrawn • unresponsive • refuses to communicate • feels rage at • ungrateful • full of pain • wants others to feel pain • dies with bravery • walks as a man to his death

Tante Lou (Grant's aunt)

Grant's Tante Lou, now in her early to mid 70s, worked in Henri Pichot's household all her life. Her best friend is Jefferson's godmother, Miss Emma Glenn. She raised Grant as his parents left him with her and moved to California during the war. She is a church-going, God-fearing woman, close to Reverend Ambrose. Her relationship with Grant is marked by bickering and sullen struggles which seem initially rather ill-tempered. Her disapproval of Grant's loss of faith and efforts to extract himself from the punishing life in the segregated South, however, mask a love for him which only occasionally surfaces. Her coolness towards Vivian is caused by her fears that she will lose Grant to the other woman; and Grant himself knows that one of the most effective weapons he has at his disposal in conflicts with his aunt is the threat of him leaving. The fact that she also uses this threat against him makes their mutual need more apparent to the reader; the two of them do love each other, despite all the hard words, glowering stares, and hurtful provocations.

Her love for Grant is neither uncomplaining nor unconditional: there is no sentimentalism in Gaines' portrayal of this character. She drives him to do what Miss Emma wants against his will (p. 76, l. 22 –

p. 75, l. 2). But what she does, she does for Grant as much as for Miss Emma or Jefferson; like Vivian, she pushes Grant to be true to himself, knowing that failure to do so would ruin him.

Key passages	
"You going with us up the quarter," my aunt said, as though I hadn't said a word. "You going up there with us, Grant, or you don't sleep in this house tonight." (p. 16, ll. 12–14)	She is a tough woman who uses threats to get her way with Grant.
"Me and Emma can make out all right without you coming through that back door ever again" (p. 19, ll. 20–21) *"It was you who said you never wanted me to go through that back door ever again"* (p. 18, ll. 12–13)	She is aware of the oppressive status quo, which is why she sent Grant away to get educated. She wants him to be a respected black man, treated as an equal by whites.
p. 107, l. 33 – p. 111, l. 34 p. 155, ll. 33–35	Her first and second meetings with Vivian illustrate her fear of losing Grant to another woman.
p. 109, ll. 1–9	She is a strategic thinker. Here she must balance three potential outcomes concerning herself, Grant, and her friends.

Emma Glenn (Miss Emma, Jefferson's godmother)

Miss Emma is a generous-spirited, strong-minded woman in her mid-70s. She has raised her godson Jefferson and worked in the Pichots' household all her life (p. 19, ll. 9–19 and p. 21, l. 20ff.). She is the person in the story who is closest to Jefferson. It is her love for him that leads to her request to Grant to teach Jefferson to walk like a man to his death (see p. 14 ll. 25–26). During Jefferson's time in the courthouse jail, she brings him food she has cooked herself, and when she doesn't go, she makes sure that Grant takes the food for Jefferson.

She suffers the most from Jefferson's pain and sullen unresponsiveness. She herself only knows one way to try to reach him – with undemanding love, a constant stream of comfort (in the form of home-cooked meals) and support. She turns to Grant and to Reverend Ambrose to accomplish that which she herself can't – Ambrose to try to save Jefferson's soul, and Grant to teach the young man to find himself (p. 22, ll. 13–21; p. 156, ll. 14–18).

Key passages	
"I don't want them to kill no hog," she said. "I want a man to go to that chair, on his own two feet." (p. 14, ll. 25–26)	Here she expresses the desire of the whole black community.
p. 23, ll. 5–10 " *'Cause somebody go'n do something for me 'fore I die*" (p. 117, l. 24)	These statements reflect a life of oppression (cf. Jefferson's statement, p. 162, ll. 25–26)
p. 13, ll. 18–19 p. 14, ll. 10–24 p. 18, ll. 17–18 p. 94, ll. 24–25 p. 153, ll. 10–13	Her frequent absences during conversations due to her emotional pain

p. 114, l. 18 – p. 117, l. 26	The disastrous visit to Jefferson is a pivotal moment for all concerned: for Miss Emma in particular, as she realizes that her undemanding love and constant supply of food – the way she knows best to offer and provide love and support – are not enough for Jefferson, that he needs more than she can give him.

Reverend Mose Ambrose

Reverend Ambrose, despite being a spiritual leader, is a simple man. Uneducated and untraveled, he initially feels himself at a loss when confronting Grant, and falls back on dire warnings against backsliding in faith. He is overwhelmed and scared by Henri Pichot's house (p. 147, l. 33 – p. 148, l. 3). Despite his intellectual limitations and inflexibility, he understands his purpose and his congregation and the role he must play for them (p. 206, ll. 11–31). His attack on Grant seems to be unfair, as Grant has already shown in his conversations with Vivian (pp. 157–160) that he fully understands the sacrifices made by the community, and the women of the quarter in particular. What Ambrose tries to explain to Grant is the need for lying; the way that lies can protect others from truths which will do them no good. This is not a positive view of religion, but for the blacks in the South it was a way to *"relieve pain"* (p. 206, l. 13).

Ambrose seems for the most part an unsympathetic character. He believes that Jefferson has greater need of him than of Grant, even though Miss Emma specifically asks the two of them to work together in trying to reach Jefferson. But the trouble is that Jefferson is much more responsive to Grant's more low-key, human appeal, and seems uninterested in his own salvation. This perceived defeat gives rise to the envy he feels towards Grant for the younger man's success in breaking through to Jefferson in his hour of greatest need (p. 185, ll. 26ff.). The matter of Jesus and Heaven seems to be secondary by this point; Ambrose's envy exposes a very basic human desire for self-importance.

Yet, throughout the novel, it is the Reverend Ambrose who stands by Miss Emma and offers support to those who need it. As he says, *"I know my people. I know what they gone through."* (p. 206, ll. 28–29). At the end, it is Reverend Ambrose whose faith and sense of duty give him the strength to attend the execution, to be with Jefferson right at the end (p. 235, l. 32 – p. 236, l. 10) and to gain from Grant the acknowledgement that *"the old man is much braver than I"* (p. 236, l. 3).

Key passages	
p. 96, ll. 8–17	Ambrose's background
p. 139, ll. 2–7	Praying for Grant as he has lost his faith
p. 172, l. 11 – p. 174, l. 31	Argument about the radio Grant bought for Jefferson, which represents worldly sins for the Reverend.
pp. 201–206	Confrontation with Grant about their different approaches to Jefferson
p. 185, ll. 11–15 p. 185, l. 26 – p. 186, l. 1	Ambrose's envy of Grant's success

Vivian Baptiste

Vivian has been Grant's girlfriend for three years (p. 29, ll. 21–22). She is a beautiful light-skinned (*"Miss Fine Brown"*, p. 26, ll. 27–28) Catholic black woman, married, but separated from her husband. She has two children, and works as a teacher in Bayonne. She comes originally from a town called Free LaCove, which has a reputation for being prejudiced against darker-skinned blacks (p. 109, ll. 21–26). However, Vivian has no such prejudices, as she married a dark-skinned black man, which resulted in her being ostracized from her family (p. 107, ll. 13–26).

Vivian embraces her culture and heritage and identifies with the black community. Both Tante Lou and Jefferson, under different circumstances, recognize in her an inherent "*quality*", marking her as a lady. Moreover, unlike Grant, she accepts her responsibilities as a mother, teacher, and lover.

She loves Grant, and this love is expressed in her caring for him (e.g. preparing food for him after the fight in the bar, pp. 194, ll. 34–36; p. 195, ll. 20–23) as well as defying his wishes (p. 28, l. 20 – p. 30, l. 3 and p. 134, ll. 1–12), and also physically (p. 103, l. 30 – p. 105, l. 11). Grant seems to be able to talk with her about almost everything, and at times is weak in front of her, the only person on whom he feels he can rely. Vivian doesn't want him to change or do something he does not want to, unlike his aunt and Reverend Ambrose; what she most wants for Grant is that he be true to himself in the long term. She does not want him to betray his principles or himself by fleeing from Bayonne. She understands as clearly as he does himself that flight would mean destroying what is good in him.

Vivian becomes pregnant during the novel, after sleeping with Grant in the cornfield (p. 104, l. 20 – p. 105, l. 8). This event finally triggers the end of her marriage, which not only means that she and Grant are now free to love each other, but that, because the husband demands that she not take the children away, she and Grant must stay in the area.

Vivian, like Tante Lou, has strong faith in Grant's potential to become more than he is, to grow out of himself and fulfill their expectations. This faith is justified by his final success in reaching Jefferson, but also by the mere act of working towards this goal. Vivian encourages Grant not only to help Jefferson become a man in spite of the white authorities' oppression, but also to become more himself than the role he is assigned as a teacher to black children in Louisiana: his self-image as someone who dispenses "*reading, writing and arithmetic*" is self-limiting, and Vivian's love and support and pride in him help Grant to accomplish the task of becoming all he can be.

Key passages	
p. 27, ll. 19–26	Description
p. 107, ll. 12–26	Her history
p. 90, l. 33 – p. 91, l. 10 p. 134, ll. 1–12	Vivian refuses to leave the area.
pp. 194–199	After the fight, Vivian cares for Grant and supports him.

Matthew Antoine

Matthew Antoine was the teacher at the plantation school when Grant was a boy. Antoine, a bitter old mulatto, now dead, only appears in one scene, a recollection of Grant's. This scene is however essential for an understanding of Grant and the themes of racism, escape, duty and responsibility in the novel. This section on pages 61 to 64 is one of the most relevant and important scenes for study in the novel. His advice to "*Just do the best you can. But it won't matter.*" (p. 64, ll. 22–23) seems to reflect Grant's state of mind, and shows the reader Grant's possible fate: one of self-hatred reflected in his contempt for the black community, as he can never be a full equal member of society.

Sam Guidry

Sam Guidry is the sheriff of the town. He is also the brother-in-law of Henri Pichot. Sheriff Guidry is consistently presented during the novel as an unpleasant man and an unsympathetic character. He is racist, callous, arrogant, and suspicious of Grant and Miss Emma. He allows Grant numerous concessions in his visits with Jefferson, the most prominent of these being the decision to allow Jefferson to meet his visitors in the spacious, furnished dayroom rather than in his cramped cell. This concession only occurs after Miss Emma's appeal – strengthened by some emotional blackmailing – to the Sheriff's wife Edna.

Sam Guidry's attitude to Grant is one of distaste and suspicion. He dislikes the mere fact that Grant is an educated black man; he is suspicious of a black man who thinks himself "*clever*" (p. 149, ll. 8–9). He repeatedly accuses Grant of deceit in his dealings, suggesting that he had provoked Miss Emma to make her request in the first place, and that he was behind the idea of using the dayroom (p. 125, l. 12 – p. 126, l. 10). This suspicion and aggressive dislike seems to mask a sense of insecurity – Grant is undoubtedly, in intellectual terms, his superior. This fact is hard for Guidry to integrate in his racist world view, in which blacks are "*niggers*" and the white race is the apex of creation. One interesting fact is that he does worry about how he is viewed, even by a black man who is to be executed: "*put that down in yo tablet i [Sheriff Guidry] tret you good all the time you been her*" (p. 221, l. 7), and shows compassion to Jefferson at the very end, perhaps also an indication that he too has become aware that Jefferson is a man.

Key passages	
p. 45, ll. 22–27	Description
p. 45, l. 32 – p. 49, l. 9 "*You're smart. Maybe you're just a little too smart for your own good.*" (p. 48, ll. 5–6)	His racist and condescending attitude to blacks is very obvious.
pp. 124–127	Sheriff Guidry summons Grant to his office to question him about his progress with Jefferson.
p. 220, l. 25 – p. 221, l. 11	Guidry's visit to Jefferson on the night before his execution: the Sheriff appears to be feeling guilty, and asks that Jefferson include positive things about him and his deputies in his diary.

Paul Bonin

Paul Bonin, the *"young deputy"*, is one of the few unreservedly positive characters in the novel. He is consistently presented as being a decent, honest, trustworthy man (p.67, ll.29–33; p.72, ll.8–9; p.119, ll.7ff.; p.161, ll.1–26). This is notable as he is not only a white man in a racially discriminating society, but he is also working in the courthouse where Jefferson is being held before his execution, thus making Paul implicitly a part of the machinery of racist and all-powerful "justice" to which Jefferson has fallen victim. The fact that he can transcend the role in which birth has placed him is a subtle ray of hope in the novel, as it foreshadows the future successes of the Civil Rights Movement. Paul and Grant exchange first names, with Grant calling him 'Paul' – as opposed to 'Mr. Paul', which is how blacks were expected to address white people. Paul's simple humanity and warmth in offering Grant his friendship (p.120, ll.8–12) provides a stable support for Grant during his visits to Jefferson. In the final chapter Paul as a white man pays Grant the respect which the latter deserves by acknowledging his talent, and at the same time offers him his friendship (p.242, l.5). Without this change in the attitudes of white people, nothing can change.

Key passages	
p.120	Offering friendship to Grant
p.239, l.9 – p.242, l.15	Coming to see Grant after the funeral

Edna Guidry (Sam's wife)

Edna Guidry is the wife of the arrogant, racist sheriff. She is not a sympathetic character, coming across as slightly foolish and insecure, as she nervously drinks bourbon in the kitchen (p.44, ll.10–12) or panics with her coffee in the living room. Her closeness to Miss Emma makes her feel sympathy for her situation, just as she does for the widow of the storekeeper: *"I'm sorry for both families."* (p.44, l.1). When the date of the execution becomes known, it is she who suggests Miss Emma may need a doctor (p.149, ll.1–2). It is thanks to her persuasiveness and diplomacy that Grant is allowed to visit Jefferson in the first place. As Inez says, *"I'm sure it's Miss Edna making him do it"* (p.45, ll.13–14). It is due to her that Jefferson is allowed access to the dayroom when receiving visitors (p.126, l.3 – p.127, l.5). Sheriff Guidry complains about this a few times, suspecting Grant of having somehow manipulated matters, but he is overlooking the basic decency which requires his wife to do what she can to help an elderly woman who has given her life in service to this family, who now have it in their power to offer whatever comfort they can in this sad and painful time. Even though Edna does not challenge the racist structures, she is able to show that the proximity between whites and blacks (even on a master-servant basis) can lead to personal attachments. This is seen most obviously when she *"set a precedent by having them [the two black ladies] sit in the living room"* (p.126, ll.13–14), where they are served coffee by the maid.

Dr. Joseph Morgan (the school inspector)

In his own way every bit as distasteful a character as Sheriff Guidry, the school inspector is a fat, lazy, arrogant white man whose purpose is simple: he wants to ensure that the black schools are kept at the lowest possible levels necessary to function. His examination of the children reminds Grant of what he has read about slave owners (p.55, ll.1–9). Education is a game the black teachers and children may dabble in, but in his view it is more important for the black children to get exercise by working out in the fields or by harvesting pecans. Reciting Bible verses and pledging allegiance to the American flag are the simple duties he expects the children to be able to master. The fact that Grant has no materials with which to teach his children is of no interest to the school inspector. He is an agent of segregation who has no interest in seeing black schools successfully educate their students. Dr. Morgan has also apparently joined in with Louis Rougon's bet that Grant will fail to prepare Jefferson in time (p.217, ll.22–25), a terrible indictment of a person responsible for education in the district.

Henri Pichot (brother-in-law to Sheriff Sam Guidry)

Henri Pichot is the owner of the plantation on which Grant was raised and where his aunt worked. His sister, Edna, is married to Sam Guidry, the Sheriff. He seems perpetually nervous or uncomfortable (p.47, ll.11–12; p.48, l.29; p.148, ll.8–9). This may be because an emotional response is due, as the blacks involved are in some way connected to his family, and because he has to deal with their needs, which is a new, unusual, and probably unpleasant experience for him. He spoke up for Jefferson during the trial, but we never learn how, or what he said. He does refuse to take part in Louis Rougon's bet that Grant will fail to prepare Jefferson for his execution (p.41, ll.22–27; p.217, ll.22–25). Henri Pichot does show some compassion for Jefferson, sharpening his pencil for him, offering to get him a new pencil, and then giving Jefferson his own pearl-handled knife.

Other characters:	
Alcee Gropé	The murdered man
Brother Bear	The two men who picked Jefferson up, and who died attempting to rob Mr Gropé's store
Joe & Thelma Clairborne	Owners of the Rainbow Club in Bayonne. They are "*good people*" (p.27, l.2), who contribute generously to the cost of the radio Grant buys for Jefferson.
Shirley	The waitress at the Rainbow Club
Louis Rougon	A banker who bets that Grant will not be able to get Jefferson ready to die. The whole business is for Rougon just entertainment – Jefferson's sentence, Miss Emma's idea for Grant, and Grant's request; it all just amuses him (p.46, ll. 24–26; p.47, ll.11–12; p.48, l l.25–28).

Farrell Jarreau	Pichot's handyman, who carries messages and is an integral part of the quarter and its daily life.
Clark (Senior deputy)	A racist white man, Paul Bonin's immediate superior, Clark is a mean-spirited, hostile man. He dislikes blacks in general and Jefferson in particular, and has a special hatred for Grant. Jefferson mistrusts him to the end (p. 217, ll. 26–29).
Inez Lane	Pichot's maid
Miss Eloise Bouie	Church-going friend of Tante Lou (first appearance on p. 92)
Irene Cole	Assistant teacher, who seems to be infatuated with Grant (pp. 157–160). She is a reliable, clever, helpful girl.
Louis Washington Jr.	Grant's most problematic pupil (p. 53, l. 32 – p. 54, l. 26)
Henry Lewis and Amos Thomas	Two black men who deliver wood to Grant's school

Structure and Language

Narration

First-person narration

The novel is narrated (almost exclusively) by the first-person narrator Grant's, which means that we get his perspective. The chapters follow a standard, chronological progression from the trial through to after Jefferson's execution. There are a few flashbacks, which are used to illustrate some element within the scenes in which they occur: for example Grant's recollections of Matthew Arnold (pp. 61–64), in the chapter describing his school and pupils; and Miss Emma's visit to Jefferson during which he refused to speak to her because he was listening to his radio (pp. 170–172). The story does not require experimental or challenging structural strategies: it describes a journey from A (the trial) to B (the execution) and is concerned with the developments along this path.

This standard structure is also found in the narrative perspective, which, with two exceptions (Chapter 29, which is Jefferson's diary, and Chapter 30, which consists of fragments of perspectives which are not Grant's), belongs to Grant. This stable (there is one single perspective) and personal (it is a narrative being recounted by a person, and not by an omniscient narrator) structure makes sense, given Grant's role as central character, observer, and initially unwilling participant in the events of the novel.

The two chapters which are exceptions to this are Chapters 29 and 30.

Chapter 29: Jefferson's diary

Chapter 29 consists of Jefferson's entries in the notebook Grant has given him. These entries include painfully developed ideas and thoughts which could not have been shown to the reader of the novel in any other way – we have seen already how Jefferson struggles to articulate himself, having to fight against not only the emotional turmoil within himself, but also against his ignorance, lack of education, and his apparent inability to understand either himself or the world around him. This last point is interesting, as it becomes clear in

Chapter 29 that Jefferson does actually understand a lot more than we, the readers, or even Grant and Miss Emma have been giving him credit for. He writes down his thoughts about various characters and situations specifically for Grant to read (p. 214, ll. 2–7, p. 216, ll. 15–22). He writes that he likes Grant, but doesn't know how to say this (p. 216, ll. 21–22) – his diary is full of such thoughts, things he would like to say or to have said but finds himself unable to express. The diary is the only way we as readers can see these thoughts of Jefferson's, and in addition, the very format (written) serves to prove how far he has come under Grant's guidance, and how far removed he is from the ignorant beast the white authorities believe him – and would like him – to be.

Chapter 30: The Morning of the Execution

Chapter 30, which follows Jefferson's diary entries, changes perspective suddenly. Within a novel which has, up to this point, been narrated by one character, it seems strange to suddenly have these texts which are obviously describing not only the situations and actions but also the feelings of other characters – things which Grant could have had no way of knowing. The sudden change to the third-person narrator can be explained as a way of showing how the execution of one man affects a whole town, or to show how people go about their business on the day of the execution. The large number of completely "*new*" characters who have not been mentioned in any way before serves to give the reader an impression of just what a big event Jefferson's execution is for the entire town of Bayonne.

Language

The language of the novel is for the most part straightforward and easy to follow. There are seldom lengthy descriptions, which is perhaps appropriate for a first-person narration. The descriptions in the novel are normally concerned with the countryside around Bayonne or with the town's structure. Gaines is writing a story to bring across his ideas about the central themes of the novel, and these aims do not require the use of dramatic stylistic devices. This restraint and discipline in the use of language and tone can be compared to the "conservative" structure of the novel.

Indeed although it is Jefferson who is suffering from a terrible injustice that will result in his execution, he himself is silent and restrained. He never cries out against his fate. All the anger is centred in Grant. Occasionally, his bitterness will manifest in sarcasm and violence directed at youngsters who cannot respond (see Chapter 5, and especially page 150). Only once does he address the injustice directly, which he does sarcastically and silently (p. 150). But the general tone of the novel, while touching on melancholy and with occasional flashes of anger or frustration, remains level-headed and undramatic.

The conversations give the reader an impression of the local dialect, and the degrees of education between Louis Washington Jr. (at one end of the spectrum, e.g. p. 54, ll. 9–26) and Vivian (at the other end – an educated woman, a woman of "*quality*"). Grant's narrative is precise and correct, suiting his character. The exceptions are, again, the two chapters towards the end, 29 and 30. Chapter 29 is of course written in Jefferson's broken, dialect-heavy English, and this chapter should ideally be read aloud to be understood; Jefferson's spelling and grammar are as bad as could be expected, and many of the spellings he uses make no sense at all when not spoken out loud.

Chapter 30 on the other hand brings very new stylistic elements. The language becomes increasingly terse as the chair is being set up in the courthouse. The sentences become shorter, adjectives more seldom, until the chapter reads like a report which has been written using the most minimal language possible while still providing the most information possible. The best example of this is the passage from p. 230, l. 10 to p. 232, l. 33. The conversations and actions are all described without any embellishment. By reporting the conversations the narrator even removes the sound of dialect and personality from the story. Only right at the end when Jefferson talks is direct speech used.

Symbolism and Imagery

Segregation

The slavery of the 18th to 19th centuries is present in the novel, despite it having long been abolished. When the black characters enter white areas – Pichot's plantation house, the courtroom – they become second-class citizens, with limited freedom of movement and expression. The kitchen door at Pichot's house symbolizes this *de facto* continuation of the segregation of society. The black characters, even those like Miss Emma who should be entitled by their age and years of service to the household to more respect, must use this side entrance to the house. Grant feels the effects of this symbolic entrance particularly strongly, understanding the humiliation and contempt it represents (p. 76, l. 22 – p. 77, l. 9). Every time he enters through the kitchen door, Grant feels his person and accomplishments diminished – his education means nothing (indeed, it becomes a problem for him, as he is better educated than the white men he encounters but must make an effort not to let them feel this) and any pride he has must be held back. The expectation is that he must behave in a submissive and grateful manner.

The visit of the school superintendent, Dr. Joseph Morgan, is an equally striking symbolic reminder of the position of blacks in this segregated society. While he is examining the children, Grant is reminded of slave masters (p. 55, ll. 4–9).

A reversal, or inversion, of the slave-associated symbolism can be found in the scene in which Vivian and Grant make love in the sugar cane field (Chapter 14). For three centuries the plantation fields and sugar cane crops have been associated with slavery, with the use by white landowners of imported black slaves to work in their fields. The fields themselves are symbolic of the contempt the whites feel for the blacks (see Dr. Morgan's suggestion that Grant send his pupils to work in the fields in order to be able to afford toothbrushes, p. 56). But when Vivian and Grant spend time in the field, they transcend these associations of oppression and slave labor; their love not only lifts them temporarily above their cares and troubles, it even leads to

Vivian's pregnancy. The field is therefore transformed from being a symbol of slavery to one of hope and life.

Objects connected with Jefferson

The symbolism of certain objects in the novel is also important. Most obvious are the notebook, the radio, and the **electric chair**. The electric chair's significance is obvious: it means death. The complexities of the issue of Jefferson's death are not touched on by the chair. It simply is, and the scenes in which it is brought into Bayonne (see Chapter 30) describe the focus it provides for the attention of the town's inhabitants (as well as providing the crucial event of the novel, Jefferson's execution). It is the culmination of the sequence of objects with which Jefferson has come into contact.

The **radio** symbolized his gradual return to "*community*", re-introducing him to the music that other people would be listening to, to voices from outside, to a sense of the shared nature of life, a life from which he has been cut off by circumstance (locked up in jail) and by his attitude (rejection of everyone around him). It is one of the stages he goes through during his time with Grant.

The **notebook** symbolizes the conclusion of Jefferson's journey; it is his legacy, the results of his attempts, guided by Grant, to discover himself in the face of death. It is a symbol of hope in various ways. Its contents show a man coming to terms with himself, overcoming ignorance and despair. It symbolizes the hope inherent in friendship – the friendship that has grown up between Jefferson and Grant. And, at the end, it provides a symbol of hope for reconciliation between whites and blacks (see p.241). Jefferson's painful struggle to express himself in the notebook is a powerful symbol of the triumph of will over adversity, both in the notebook's contents as well as in the language, clumsy and incorrect yet bursting with the force of what Jefferson is trying to express.

Religion

The religious imagery becomes increasingly important as the novel progresses. The identification of Jefferson with Jesus is rooted in the date set for his execution – Easter. The concrete presence of *"religion"* in the novel – in the form of Reverend Ambrose – is not positive, but the symbolism is more interesting. Grant's school, itself symbolizing hope and the potential for change and a better life, is in an old church, combining the practical hopes of an education with the spiritual hopes of faith. The efforts his students make in their Christmas program also symbolize hope – the Christmas message – for the community. The identification of Jefferson with Jesus allows this simple character to embody the huge issues which are tackled in the novel: standing up straight in the face of oppression and death and the hope for a *"savior"* (the focus for hope) who can break the vicious cycle of black submission to white dominance, and the promise of a better world to come.

Animals

The single most important use of symbolism in the novel is however the ***"hog"***. From the first use of this word (in the first chapter, Jefferson's defence lawyer's plea), it provides the motor for the novel. The unthinking equation of Jefferson with a beast – a beast universally associated with dirt and uncleanliness – is a potent symbol of the contempt of dominant white culture for the black community. The point of the novel, both in the plot and in the underlying message, is that Jefferson must transcend this symbol; he must prove to himself, to his loved ones, and also to the white authorities who have condemned him to death for a crime he didn't commit, that he is a man and not a beast. Because Jefferson is obviously enough a human being and not an animal, this entire topic is on a symbolic level. It is concerned with the concrete rejection of enforced expectations. Jefferson's assumption of the role of "hog" (as in the scene in which he tips his food onto the floor and buries his face in it) is an expression of pain, despair, and self-loathing. The novel charts Jefferson's growth from this resigned acceptance of his inferior status to his eventual reconciliation with himself and his fate. His death as a *"man"* destroys the racist expectations that he will die a beast (e.g. the bet made by the white men about Grant's chances of success in helping Jefferson). The equation of blacks with beasts can also be seen in the chapter about Matthew Arnold (p.61, ll.7-11).

Other incidents of animal symbolism in the novel include the **birds** in the sycamore tree visible from Jefferson's jail cell window, which symbolize the freedom he has lost, and a freedom he would never have been able to attain as a black man in Louisiana in the 1940s. This freedom – freedom from all earthly concerns – is finally symbolized by the **butterfly** (p.238, ll.10-25) which Grant observes flying away at the moment of Jefferson's death.

Themes

Racial Hierarchies

The chief deputy could see that I didn't like him, and I could tell he didn't like me. But he knew who was in charge and that I would have to take anything he dished out.
p.68, ll.3-5

According to the dictionary, racism is 1: "*the unfair treatment of people who belong to a different race; violent behaviour towards them*" or 2: "*the belief that some races of people are better than others*" (Oxford Advanced Learner's Dictionary). The first definition describes the active phenomenon, and the second the reasoning behind it. The roots of the racism described in *A Lesson Before Dying* lie in the history of European exploration of Africa, and the slave trade. Racism itself is as old as mankind, and examples can be found in the Bible as well as in Greek and Roman history (both civilizations drew strict lines between their respective citizens and "*barbarians*", who were accorded lower status and fewer rights in society) and the ancient histories of cultures as diverse as those of India, China and Japan.

Slavery in the United States lasted from the 17th century until 1865, when the 13th Amendment to the Constitution prohibited slavery. It is estimated that around 12 million Africans were brought to North America as slaves during this period. Following the Civil War (1861-1865), during the Reconstruction Period (1865-1877), slavery was abolished, but only in a *de jure* sense: the *de facto* conditions for most blacks, especially in the South, had very little to do with freedom. Generations of white property owners (for example, Henri Pichot) had become accustomed to being a ruling class by virtue of their race, and generations of blacks had become resigned to living in a state of uneducated poverty (for example, Jefferson). Between these two extremes were the gray areas of poor whites, people of mixed race ("*mulattoes*", e.g. Grant's old teacher, Matthew Antoine), differing degrees of "*blackness*" (in Vivian's home town), and educated blacks (Grant).

These different layers of the racist society described in the novel constitute a hierarchy of race, which is a topic in *A Lesson Before Dying*. It can be seen in numerous situations: the segregation of the town of Bayonne; the trial; the Sheriff's behaviour and the jail routines; Pichot's household; Grant's old teacher; the fight with the mulattoes in the bar; and Vivian's home town.

The Town

Bayonne is described by Grant on pp.24–25. The town is segregated: the riverside establishments are for the whites, while the poor quality clubs are for the black population. There are separate churches for blacks and whites, a cinema for whites in town and a black cinema out of town. The "*colored section*" is outside the town, and is reached by an "*unlit road*" (p.25, l.17). The message is clear – the whites don't want to have to see or deal with blacks more than is absolutely necessary, and the blacks should not become accustomed to sharing facilities with the white population.

The black quarters in rural Louisiana were marked by poverty.

The Justice System

For Jefferson and the people in the quarter, the trial is decided before it has even begun (p.5, ll.1–2, p.6, ll.1–4, p.12, ll.4–5). A white judge and a jury of twelve white men sentence a black man to death (as Grant summarizes on p. 150 ll. 12–33). The central argument in the defense lawyer's plea (p. 8, l. 28 – p. 10, l. 25) is that Jefferson is subhuman, and therefore incapable of planning or committing a crime. It is this dehumanizing argument - that Jefferson is a "*hog*" and not a man - more than the sentence itself, which upsets Miss Emma. What Grant objects to is the fact that a black man is tried, judged, and sentenced exclusively by white people.

The officials and routines in the courthouse jail are further examples of the hierarchy of racial discrimination. Sheriff Guidry and his chief deputy, Clarke, make no effort to hide their contempt for Jefferson and their dislike of Grant (p. 68, ll. 3–5). Guidry dislikes Grant for his cleverness (p. 46, ll. 2–5 and ll. 29–30; p. 48, ll. 5–6; p. 183, ll. 8–11). Grant knows this, and understands that an educated black man is something that the white authorities don't like, trust or understand. The underlying racist theory, that black people are inherently inferior to whites, has difficulty dealing with a man like Grant, who seems to be much better educated than Guidry, for example. It is clear in the interactions between Grant and Guidry that the white sheriff expects a certain kind of behavior from blacks, and this behavior should be submissive and deferential. The sheriff makes it very clear that, left to his own devices, he would not have allowed the visits to take place; the concessions Guidry makes to Miss Emma and Grant – the visits, the radio, and the dayroom – are pressured out of him by his wife Edna (sister to the plantation owner Henri Pichot).

The jail itself is segregated, reinforcing the hierarchy of race – for example, the toilets for blacks are in a terrible state, and are in the cellar (p.66 l.30 – p.67 l.2). The white toilets are in the courthouse building. The jail cells for black and white prisoners are segregated (p.68 ll.18-19). The reader, like Grant and Miss Emma, never encounters a white prisoner.

The Plantation House

The other white-dominated environment in the novel is Henri Pichot's house. Grant grew up around the house, as his aunt worked there (p. 19, ll. 5–25). The house represents the power and status of the plantation owner, and at the same time the dominance of the white populace in this time and place. When Miss Emma and Grant visit the house, they must wait in the kitchen; when Grant goes there alone to speak to Pichot and Guidry, he is kept waiting for over two hours. It

A typical Southern plantation house

seems like no opportunity is spared to show blacks where they stand in the hierarchy: there is not even a minimal concession to the requirements of gallantry regarding age and gender (in the case of the elderly Miss Emma, cf. p. 20, ll. 31–2).

A Vicious Circle of Poverty and Hopelessness

The theme of racial hierarchy is most explicitly and intensively dealt with in Grant's recollections of his old teacher, Matthew Antoine, in Chapter 8. Grant is watching his pupils cutting up the firewood for the school for winter, and is reminded of his own school days (p. 60, ll. 29–30). He wonders why he is trying to teach the children when all they are doing is manual labor, no different from the two old men who had brought the wood to the school that morning: "*They are fifty years younger, maybe more, but doing the same thing those old men did who never attended school a day in their lives*" (p. 60, ll. 21–23). He thinks of his own school days, and of his fellow pupils from back then, and his conclusions are bleak: those who left, died (p. 61, ll. 1–5); and those who stayed "*simply died slower*" (p. 61, l. 6).

Antoine had predicted this: *"He had told us then that most of us would die violently, and those who did not would be brought down to the level of beasts"* (p.61, ll.9–11). This idea of a vicious circle is central to the novel, with Grant as the walker in both worlds. He has experienced the outside world at university and with his parents in California, but has always returned to Bayonne. In this chapter his experiences are contrasted sharply with Antoine's, who saw himself as being *"living testimony of someone who should have run"* (p.61, l.12). The fact that he didn't leave Bayonne is understood by Antoine himself and by Grant as cowardice. This cowardice breeds hatred: *"As clearly as anything, he showed his hatred for himself, and for us"* (p.61, ll.17–18).

Antoine's message is, broadly speaking, flee or die. He applies this to all his students and expects that they will stay in Bayonne and live like beasts (cf. the primary issue of the novel's plot - Jefferson being

characterized as a *"hog"*). The exception is Grant. He tells Grant that he wants to teach him, so that Grant can then leave Bayonne and make a decent life for himself elsewhere. But, when he sees that Grant is ready to learn, he hates him even more than he does the other students. He sees Grant's desire to learn as a personal challenge to his cynical prediction that they will all fail or die, but there is also a racial element to his bitterness. As a mulatto – of mixed white and black parentage – he sees himself as being "*above*" the blacks in the hierarchy.

The Mulattoes

The mulattoes have an even more difficult role in society than blacks. They are hardly more accepted by whites than are blacks, yet they feel themselves superior to blacks due to their white heritage. Antoine explicitly admits (p.63, l.8 – p.64, l.4) that only in the South could he have felt superior to so many – anywhere else in America at the time he would have been lower down the hierarchy. In states where blacks were not subject to the segregation of the South he would not have been able to use his lighter skin color to place himself above them.

Antoine's self-hatred as a person of mixed European and African parents embodies in a tragic manner the racial divisions of this era. Whites and blacks are opposed along racist lines, and the old mulatto Antoine carries this conflict inside himself. His unspoken message to Grant and his other pupils is that they will fail - which would confirm his own hatred of not only his own nature, but all around him, as well as confirming his own feeling of racial superiority to blacks. The idea of one of these black children actually achieving what he has failed to achieve himself is, for him, a terrible prospect. He clings to his white side, as it is for him the "*superior*" side, and appears to be unable to feel pride or hope in one of his black pupils – Grant – going on to accomplish greater things. This self-negation, or rather, negation of half of himself, causes the deadly hatred which consumes him even up to his death. His last words are a display of despair and futility (p.64 ll.5–23): he tells Grant that all his efforts will be for nothing, that nothing matters anymore. Having been unable to see any signs of hope in Grant, and having been unable to rise above the racial divisions he carries within himself, Antoine dies in the most hopeless and saddest way possible. This example of a "*bad death*" - unreconciled, hopeless, broken – gives an underlying urgency and emotional intensity to Grant's efforts to help Jefferson find a "*good death*".

A later scene (in Chapter 25) involving mulattoes gives a further, brutal example of the mechanisms and consequences of the racial hierarchy in the world portrayed in the novel. While Grant is waiting in the Rainbow Club for Vivian, elated that he has finally got through to Jefferson, he becomes aware of a couple of mulatto bricklayers talking loudly about Jefferson in a derogatory manner.

Grant understands that the mulattoes in Bayonne do anything to keep away from the blacks – dropping out of school early, taking hard work in construction - *"dumb as hell, but prejudiced as hell"* (p. 187, ll. 28–9). Their hatred for the blacks is like Antoine's, only more extroverted. As an educated man, Antoine is able to at least partially understand the conflicts within himself. But the two men in the bar in this scene are deeply ignorant, and seem to be intent on provoking and insulting Grant by speaking offensively about Jefferson.

Another example of the prejudices of Mulattoes can be seen at the Christmas program at Grant's school. Grant mentions a mulatto man from the quarter called James Lavonia (p. 137). His wife Julia is in the audience; their two children are both in the Nativity play, one playing a shepherd, and the daughter playing Mary. James is, however, not present: *"he had told me once that he had better things to do than go to a coon gathering"* (p. 137, ll. 22–23) - *"coon"* is an old-fashioned, derogatory term for blacks.

Different Shades of Black

A further example of the racist hierarchy depicted in the novel is seen indirectly in Vivian's background. The blacks of her home town, Free LaCove, have a reputation for being prejudiced against darker-skinned African Americans, as Tante Lou mentions (p. 109, ll. 21–26). Vivian herself is light-skinned and had had trouble with her family when she introduced her husband, who is dark-skinned (p. 107, ll. 13–23). Vivian here serves as a fine example in the novel of what Gaines admires – someone who is able to transcend these color-lines which are enforced from above. Her first husband is darker than her, and causes difficulties between her and her family; but Grant is also much darker than she is, and again she is not prepared to let color distinctions and prejudices influence her decisions. Being in a position in which she could use her own color to place herself above those around her – as Antoine has done, for example – she chooses not to.

The hierarchy of race from white down to black causes this racist attitude to be handed down even among the blacks. Black is bad: the blacker the skin, the lower the man (or woman). This phenomenon is not limited to the American South or to the USA but it is an issue which Gaines specifically confronts in his novel. In American society, this would only be challenged following the Civil Rights Movement of the 1960s, when the concepts of *"black is beautiful"* and Black Pride were developed, and the concept of African origins began to be understood as a rich heritage, rather than a distasteful burden.

Communication

Frequently during the novel characters communicate without speaking. Things are left unsaid, yet are understood: messages are given with glances and minimal gestures. This happens in various situations, between various characters, and to various purposes. It can quite often be understood as Gaines' expression of simple humanity, the need to console or be comforted (p.72, ll.8–9; p.232, ll.30–33; p.166, l.27 – p.167, l.6); or of an inability to articulate and express complex or painful issues and matters (p.14, ll.28–31; p.40, ll.20–26; p.145, l.14 – p.146, l.13); or of the crippled ability to communicate within an oppressed minority which gives rise to a mutual understanding of shared suffering and injustice.

This latter interpretation is the most elusive. The communities Gaines is describing in the novel are living in the shadow of three centuries of slavery. The black population in the South had been denied access to education or culture for hundreds of years. The concrete effects of this include the unwillingness and inability to communicate freely and openly – for fear of saying things which might be overheard by the wrong people, or of saying things which might worsen an already bad situation. An example of this kind of unspoken communication in the novel can be found on p.71, ll.5–11 and ll.22–23. Jefferson here exemplifies both aspects: as an uneducated person, he is unable to articulate certain things – and he and Grant, sharing a similar background, can communicate attitudes or understandings to each other by the merest suggestion. In this case Jefferson, for whatever reason, is unwilling to speak explicitly to Miss Emma about his impending execution, but knows that Grant understands exactly what he is talking about.

The novel opens with an example of things being known while remaining unsaid (p. 5, ll. 1-2). The shared experience and understanding of their situation among the people of the black quarter make speaking about certain things irrelevant. No one needs to have been present at Jefferson's trial to have learned what the outcome was going to be: experience has taught them that there will be no surprises when a black man is accused of having killed a white man. This shared understanding can transport different emotions and feelings: it can lead to a sense of despair and futility, as in the case of the opening of the novel, or it can carry the warmth of unspoken compassion and consolation, as with Inez Lane's quiet understanding of Grant's humiliation and frustration at being made to wait in Pichot's kitchen.

As an issue in the novel this is relevant, as a large part of Grant's work with Jefferson is to make the younger man understand complex and abstract matters (dignity, love, defiance of the status quo, hope) which are implicitly felt and more or less understood by both of them, but which must be made real in order to help Jefferson approach his death in the way his godmother wishes – to put that which goes unsaid into words.

Men and women

The theme of the relationship between men and women is dealt with explicitly in the novel in one key conversation between Grant and Vivian (in Chapter 21, pp. 157–160), which brings together implicit issues from throughout and links the roles of men and women to other major themes from the novel, such as racism, escape, and hope.

They have gone to the Rainbow Club after having visited Miss Emma, who has taken to her bed after hearing that the date has been set for Jefferson's execution. Meetings between Vivian and the other women in Grant's life have been prickly with tension so far; she especially feels a certain coldness from Irene Cole (Grant's assistant teacher; p. 156, ll. 1–3) and Tante Lou (p. 108, l. 1 – p. 111, l. 32). As they sit in the bar and drink, Grant explains to her his theories about men and women in the quarter, and, in general terms, throughout the segregationist society of the American South.

Grant explains that what Vivian perceives as coldness is merely the fear among the women that *"an outsider"* is going to take him away from them. This fear, he says, comes from the fact that people want to hold on to *"a local boy"* because they have so little of anything and everything else.

Vivian's insistence that Irene is in love with Grant in a way confirms what he says, because she is herself exhibiting this kind of jealous possessiveness. But what he is talking about is actually bigger than this. His argument is in three parts; a personal, specific part; then more general; and then specifically personal again.

He argues that what his aunt and Irene want from him, as a young black man in their lives in this time and place, is the same as what Miss Emma wants from Jefferson: memories, and something to be proud of. This idea has been present throughout the novel in the task Miss Emma has set Grant – to help Jefferson become a man. It becomes, in this conversation, specifically linked to the roles of men and women. Grant mentions here that Reverend Ambrose, his counterpart in the struggle for Jefferson, cannot give Miss Emma what she wants. The efforts they are making for Jefferson are not confined to his soul, or to the religious and spiritual dimensions of his death: *"No, she wants memories, memories of him standing like a man"* (p. 158, ll. 34–35).

The reasoning behind this is not clear to Vivian, so Grant begins to explain it again, in broader terms: *"We black men have failed to protect our women since the time of slavery"* (p. 159, ll. 3–4). In this section he comes back yet again to the vitally important theme of escape: that the options for black men are to stay and be broken, or to run away. The new element here is the idea that running away – which has in other treatments of this topic in the novel been more linked to the cycle of violence and death which awaits black men from the South in the cities and the North – means leaving something behind. In this case, it is the women who are left behind. What Grant clearly states here – that the women are left alone *"to look after the children and themselves"* (p. 159 l. 6) – has been implicit in the novel. The black women in the book are almost all alone. Tante Lou is unmarried; Miss Emma is widowed; Irene Cole, Inez Lane, and Eloise Bouie are all single. The only exceptions are Thelma Clairborne (who is happily married) and Vivian (who is caught between two men, Grant and her husband). Jefferson's father is entirely absent, and he was raised by Miss Emma, just as Grant was raised by his aunt after his parents left for California.

Fathers in general are conspicuous in their absence in the novel. The exceptions are ghostly: Grant in a way assumes the role of substitute father (a guiding role model) for Jefferson, and this role is reflected in his own impending, very real fatherhood, when he learns that Vivian is pregnant.

This absence of men in the black community (absence in the sense of either having left, or having stayed as broken men) is the reason for the possessiveness he and Vivian had been talking about - *"each time a male child is born, they [the women] hope he will be the one to change this vicious circle – which he never does"* (p.159, ll.6–8). Grant believes that no one can make this change happen because of the burden of all those who have failed before. This failure to be able to provide what the women want and need from him will make *"the black man"* want to run away in order to stay sane – this is the vicious circle.

Grant makes the discussion specific again by mentioning what he believes Miss Emma wants from Jefferson: *"what she wants to hear first is that he did not crawl to the white man, that he stood at that last moment and walked. Because if he does not, she knows that she will never get another chance to see a black man stand for her"* (p.159 ll.18-21). Jefferson is the last chance for Miss Emma to feel hope for the future – he is her chance to see the beginning of a change in the way black people have lived for the past three hundred years (see p.159 ll.13-14). All that she can do for Jefferson is provide love and support (see the discussion below of comfort, food and family). It is up to Grant – another focal figure for the hopes of the black women in the quarter – to help Jefferson realize this potential as a symbol or hope and change.

And, bringing their conversation full circle, Grant points out to Vivian that it is he who must fill this role for his aunt. Having never married, she has no husband or sons or grandsons in whom she can invest her love and hope and pride. She and Irene, as well as other women in the quarter, are surrounded by the broken men who have failed to escape. Grant is saying that the men who remain in Bayonne are the failures; just like Antoine said they would be. Grant stands as a stark contrast to the other black men: he is articulate, educated, young, intelligent. He is an obvious focus for all their hopes. But in order for him to fulfill their expectations he must stay, and if he stays he will be broken like all the others before him. The vicious circle appears again as a theme which denies the men the opportunity to be free, and the women the chance to see their men (husbands, fathers, sons) live decent lives.

Teaching

The theme of teaching is present throughout the novel, in the title, in the main character's profession, and in the central matter, the teaching of Jefferson. The greatest danger to the black population in the novel is ignorance; it is the cause of Jefferson's trouble in the first place and is also his defence lawyer's argument. Grant's old teacher, Matthew Antoine, understands that the only possible escape for a bright boy like Grant is to educate himself in order to be able to escape the South. Grant himself is bitter and frustrated with his work as a teacher. Of the many obstacles in his path, including the poverty of the school and the troubled backgrounds of many of his students, it is the superintendent for schools in the area, Dr Joseph Morgan, who makes the whole misery most apparent. The chapter (Chapter 7, pp. 50–57) in which he appears (he is only mentioned once more, briefly, in Jefferson's notebook as having also taken part in the bet on whether or not Grant will succeed in preparing Jefferson for his execution) makes plain the terrible state of education for a segregated minority. He is uninterested in Grant and his school to such a degree that he can't even remember Grant's name; he is lazy, complaining about how much work he has to do (visiting twelve schools in total once a year). What becomes clear during his visit to the school, however, is much worse. Dr Joseph doesn't expect the children to actually learn anything, he is only concerned that they are more or less presentable while he is there – examining their hands and teeth in a manner which makes Grant think of slave-owners (p. 55, ll. 4–9) – and that they are able to recite the pledge of allegiance (a statement of loyalty to the flag which American schoolchildren are required to recite every morning). Grant's impression is that Dr Joseph is "*satisfied*" when the black children perform poorly during his inspection (p. 54, ll. 27–28). He doesn't expect the black pupils to be profiting from their education; he doesn't even want them to. He lectures the children on nutrition and advises Grant to put them to work in the fields if they need to earn money to buy toothbrushes or more materials for the school.

Education for blacks had been made possible by legislation, but the fact of segregation made it impossible in this era to provide decent education – the *de facto* effect of the education system for blacks is basically the suppression of the right, the duty, the ability, and the will to learn. A lack of material requirements – buildings, books, chalk and pencils, trained teachers and money – combines with more dangerous issues to make the education of blacks a pointless exercise; the efforts of the white authorities to keep the black population ignorant on the one hand, and on the other, the resignation and resulting lack of interest in learning on the part of the blacks. Why should blacks make the effort to have their children educated when their children will have no prospects for a future in which an education is important? The lack of opportunities for educated blacks in the world depicted in the novel diminishes the importance of education. This is entirely in the interests of the white authorities because, on a practical level, it keeps the black population helpless and dependent, while on a more abstract level is makes it easier for the upper levels of the racial hierarchy to look down on the blacks as being intellectually and socially inferior, even subhuman, thus justifying and perpetuating their racist cultural dominance.

Grant sees this hopeless prospect when he watches his own students spending their school time cutting wood for the winter (p. 60, ll. 20–24). The difficulties of his role as a teacher in such an apparently hopeless situation is evident in the use of the term "*the burden*" (p. 62, ll. 4–6) to describe it. Towards the end of the novel, Grant has accepted the role he must play as a teacher in the South in this era: he may hate the conditions he has to work under, but he has accepted who he is, and uses himself in conversation with Jefferson, much as Antoine did with him, as a negative example of the way the system works (p. 181, l. 32 – p. 182, l. 3; p. 182, ll. 17–23).

Justice

The theme of justice (and the judicial system) is equally central to the novel, forming the core matter of the plot. Grant's thoughts on *"justice"* are bitter – it is perceived as being exclusively *"white man's justice"*, intended for the protection of whites, and controlled and executed by whites. Grant is furious at the fact that Jefferson was tried, convicted and sentenced exclusively by whites. As a black man having been convicted of a crime against a white man he has no chance of mercy or fair treatment. Grant's most explicit thoughts on justice can be found in Chapter 20, on page 150. It is clear here that Grant is not only angry at the racism in the system, but is also opposed to the death penalty (p. 150, ll. 7–9).

The term *"justice"* can refer to both a legal system, and to the quality of being fair and reasonable. The second meaning is more relevant to the novel (which is after all neither a courtroom drama nor a crime thriller), and can be seen in the treatment of Jefferson as well as in the broader themes of racism and segregation. There seems to be little that is either fair or reasonable in the treatment of Jefferson; while he may have been stupid and have behaved unfortunately, he was not responsible for the deaths of Mr Gropé (or of Brother or Bear). He has been seized upon as the next best person who can be made responsible for the crime, as Brother and Bear both died during the incident. Blame and responsibility have been transferred to him to allow the justice system to punish a black man for the murder of a white man. As Grant points out right at the beginning of the novel, there is no doubt about what the result of the trial will be; the workings of the justice system are defective, and are used to satisfy the demands of a racially segregated society. There is no evidence at all against Jefferson, apart from his mere presence in the store where the crime occurred.

There is nothing the black characters in the novel can do to fight against this justice system. All they can do is help Jefferson go to his death in a manner which will allow himself and his loved ones to have some pride in him. Justice, like education, is a white man's game – it serves to maintain the racial hierarchy by protecting whites and keeping blacks down.

Religion

"it look like the lord just work for wite folks"
(p.215, l.9)

Religion is a difficult issue in the novel. Neither Grant nor Jefferson, the two main characters, have any strong religious feelings, and neither of them attend church. Neither of them find comfort in the promises of a better world to come. The function of religion as a comforter is accepted by many of the women in the novel (from Tante Lou's enthusiastic singing in church to Vivian's Catholicism). Religion offers them a sense of community and comfort. The young black men, facing so much despair and hopelessness in the segregationist South, can find no comfort or hope in the promise of a better world to come after death. Grant believes in God, and Jefferson is increasingly fascinated by Jesus, but neither can believe in the concept of Heaven. Religion is for the whites (*"their God"*, p.236, l.7; cf. also p.237, l.31 – p.238, l.6).

Religion is too abstract for Jefferson. It requires him to grasp concepts like *"the soul"* and *"Heaven"*, which have no practical application and require an effort of mind and faith on the part of the believer. As we see in the novel, he comes closer to the figure of Jesus, but largely through a realization of certain parallels and echoes of Jesus' death in his own experience. He seems to need the identification with his own life and experience to be able to develop a sense of religion and belief. Reverend Ambrose's uneducated, community-oriented religious beliefs on the other hand require religious activity: his congregation must pray and sing and attend church, they must live their religion in the community of the church. His disapproval of Grant's *"backsliding"* is frequently expressed and he demands, at least in the early days of Grant's visits to Jefferson, that Grant teach Jefferson about God. He hates the radio (the *"sin box"*) that Jefferson has in his cell and says that what he actually needs is a Bible. But Grant understands that what Jefferson most needs is human contact; religion, as it is dealt with in the novel, is on the one hand an abstract promise of hope and salvation to come after the suffering and pain of life on Earth, and on the other hand a system of community in which Jefferson, locked up in his jail cell, can take no part. Jefferson's significance in the novel has little to do with classic, Church-oriented ideas of religion, and is more symbolic, related to ideas of salvation and redemption which are partially identified with Jesus but have a much deeper relevance to the practical and immediate needs of the black community.

Community: rights, duties and responsibilities

The theme of community in the novel is evident in many ways. There are community events, such as the Christmas program, the Determination Sunday meetings in the church, and the congregation itself; and there is an effort to hold together in the face of adversity, which can be seen in the way Grant expects his pupils to be thinking about Jefferson, and, towards the end, when the pupils visit Jefferson in jail (recounted in Jefferson's journal). The community is close-knit due to segregation; the racist structures mean that the whites and the blacks are separated in their communities. These communities each bring with them their own sets of rights, duties and responsibilities, and at times these blur the color boundary. This can be seen most clearly in the character of Edna Guidry, sister of Henri Pichot, the plantation owner, and wife of Sam Guidry, the town's Sheriff.

Miss Emma appeals to Edna (and Henri) on a couple of occasions and asks her to intervene with her husband. These appeals are strengthened by the responsibility and duty Edna Guidry feels towards the old woman who had worked in the Pichot household her entire life. Edna's efforts to help Miss Emma imply different things. Does she feel guilty? Does she actually feel responsible for the black servants who had enabled her family to live in such luxury? Does she act out of simple human kindness? The truth seems to be a combination of all these things. When Emma appeals to her (p. 125–126) Edna develops a "*splitting headache*" and is troubled and uncomfortable with the situation. As a white woman – coming from a plantation-owning family – she is high up in the racial hierarchy, which has served to suppress and to a point dehumanize black people; but, having grown up with these black women all around her, making her life comfortable, cooking for her and cleaning and probably partially raising her, she is unable to treat Miss Emma with the contempt with which, for example, her husband Sam Guidry treats Grant and Jefferson. Edna's discomfort stems from this dilemma, that on the one hand she must maintain her position in the hierarchy, yet at the same time she feels a humane compulsion to assist the old woman. These bonds come from the mingling of blacks and whites within a community, albeit on different social levels.

The bonds of community are also evident in Grant's situation. The pressure put on him by his aunt are expressions of a communal need to help one of their own. His duties as a teacher are of a communal nature, not just professional. His own inner struggle – the ambivalence of his desire to escape Bayonne coupled with his complex need to stay – is connected with the theme of community. His knowledge of Bayonne (seen in his knowledge of his pupils' backgrounds and his detailed descriptions of Bayonne – the most detailed and descriptive passages in the novel) suggests his strong bonds to the community.

Other examples include the appeal to the audience at the Christmas program to think about Jefferson during the festive season (p. 114); the Clairbornes' readiness to contribute to the cost of the radio for Jefferson (p. 165); Grant's recollections of the boxing matches between Joe Louis and Max Schmeling and the euphoria in the black community at the time.

Food, family and love

Closely linked to the theme of community is the broad theme of comfort, which can be used as an umbrella term to cover the major themes of family, food and love.

Families are a difficult issue in the book. Grant's parents have left him in the care of his aunt; Jefferson's family appears to have been reduced to one person, his godmother; Vivian's family is broken and fraught with tension; and the role of men in this society (see above) has led to the general decay of family structures. The white families on the other hand are stable and complete. Those bonds which are left among the families in the black community are strong. Grant and his aunt have a difficult relationship, but it is obviously very deep and very strong; they are quick to hurt each other in their arguments and disagreements, but it is important to note that the most powerful threat either of them use is to leave the other, revealing a mutual need.

The theme of food is present throughout the novel. Food is of course the life-giver, one of the most basic and essential requirements of life; it is also in the novel symbolic of love, nurture, care, comfort. The black women in the novel are constantly cooking for their men; Tante Lou and Vivian for Grant (of especial relevance here is Chapter 16, following the fight in the bar, during which Vivian prepares food for the injured and ashamed Grant), Miss Emma for Jefferson, Inez Lane for anyone who enters her kitchen. The most important aspect of this theme is the food which Miss Emma prepares for Jefferson, and which Grant brings to him in jail (described first on p. 67).

The food symbolizes the love and support of Miss Emma for Jefferson: it is the most elemental support she can provide for him, and the most eloquent means of expressing her love for him. It comes with no strings attached: she expects nothing in return. But it still creates problems. Firstly, Grant has to undergo a humiliating process of being searched every time he goes to the jail, and the food is also unwrapped and examined every time. What is worse is the way that Jefferson constantly refuses the food. He always says that he is not hungry; Grant is unable to tempt him to try the food, which is later distributed amongst the other prisoners (or "*children*" as Miss Emma calls them, further highlighting the mother-like urge to provide and nurture those in need). The rejection of food is always a hurtful act in the novel (p. 129, ll. 27–32 and p. 24, ll. 8–9. The giver (Tante Lou or Miss Emma in these cases) wishes to provide comfort and express love in the form of food, and the rejection is understood as a rejection of comfort and love. For Miss Emma this rejection is deeply painful, as Jefferson is thereby rejecting her efforts to help him in the only way available to her. Conversely, the sharing of food has obvious Christian overtones and suggestions of the breaking of bread as a ritual expressing community and love, and can provide startlingly moving moments in the novel, for example Jefferson's gratitude for the pecans and peanuts Grant's pupils gather for him (p. 177, l. 14 – a moment of deep satisfaction for Grant, showing as it does how he has finally reached Jefferson) and his offering Grant some of his own food (p. 213 – a subtle and moving moment of reversal in which it is Jefferson who offers Grant kindness and support).

Miss Emma's efforts to get Jefferson permission to meet his visitors in the dayroom is also an effort to provide something like a proper meal situation, in which she, Tante Lou, Jefferson, Ambrose and Grant can sit and eat together, a situation which – if it had worked, which it unfortunately doesn't – would have had a symbolic value for all concerned which would have gone beyond the act of eating and encompassed the deeper comfort of a family environment.

The sharing of food provides a bond; this can also be seen in one of Grant's most lonely and despairing moments, after the Christmas program when he is sitting alone. His aunt sends a child to him with food; again, this is an unspoken expression of love and support (p. 144, ll. 13–19).

Beyond this symbolic value, food is a source of pleasure. The descriptions of food are rich, like Grant's descriptions of Bayonne itself, and Jefferson's delight at the prospect of having ice cream for his last meal (p. 162, l. 30 – p. 163, l. 9) is a rare moment of simple joy in the book.

The culmination of this theme is Jefferson's last meal (p. 220, ll. 14–21) – which he describes himself as the best meal his godmother could cook. His acceptance of his godmother's food as his final meal is a sign of his love for her.

The theme of food is largely an expression of love in the novel, of kinds of love which cannot be expressed in words for whatever reason. The central love is that of Miss Emma for Jefferson – it creates the story. It is unconditional love, but she wants something in return; she wants Jefferson to stand up straight and make her proud. Her love makes her vulnerable – she suffers greatly under Jefferson's confused, sullen behavior – but it also gives her strength.

Escape

The desire to escape is a strong theme in the novel, and is mostly connected with Grant. The pressures and hopelessness of life for black people in the South in this era led to what became known as the "*great migration*" (p. 19, ll. 26–34 and p. 235, ll. 1–9), and as a consequence has also led to the weakening of family structures, the absence of male role models, and the gradual erosion of pride and self-respect in those who remain. This bigger picture is the background to Grant's own feelings. Having been taught as a child by Matthew Antoine that his only hope in life is to educate himself and escape from Bayonne, Grant has a strong desire to leave (p. 87, ll. 17–20). What keeps him in Bayonne is a sense of commitment (p. 28, l. 20 – p. 29, l. 20) and love (p. 90, l. 33 – p. 91, l. 10). His urge to escape is great but Vivian refuses to leave with him; not just because she wants him to stay in Bayonne, but because she doesn't want him to run away from responsibilities and problems which would otherwise haunt him for the rest of his life. When she persuades him not to abandon hope and his duty to his aunt and to Jefferson, she is doing it out of love for him (p. 134, ll. 1–9).

Vivian points out to him at the end of Chapter 12 that he doesn't leave because his love (for his community) is stronger than his hatred (for the white community). He fears that his reasons for not escaping have more to do with cowardice than with love – he is probably thinking here of Antoine. The old man's self-hatred was fuelled by a sense of his own cowardice for not having left (pp. 60–64 for the passages about Antoine). Antoine's reasons for staying are unpleasant – he needs to feel superior to the blacks in the South, and as a mulatto in the North he would have no racial hierarchy in which to place himself, he would be unable to use racist structures to assert his own feelings of superiority. His cowardice is seen in the lack of confidence and respect for himself, which ultimately make him stay in Bayonne. Grant's cowardice would actually lie in running away, not in staying, as Vivian makes him understand. His commitments as a teacher are understood as being more than just professional duties – he knows the children he is teaching, he knows their families, he understands who they are and where they come from, and this knowledge and commitment make him a part of the community in the same way that Reverend Ambrose is. Escape, he knows, would ruin him, as it would entail a denial of his responsibilities and would be an act of selfishness and weakness. Strength lies in resisting the desire to escape, however strong and rational it may appear.

The threat of death and violence hangs like a cloud over the idea of escape from the South. Grant lists for himself old fellow pupils of his who met violent ends after having left Bayonne (p. 60, l. 29 – p. 61, l. 6). His dilemma, though, is not his fear of this grim prospect – what he fears is that if he stays, as his aunt (representing the black community as a whole) wants him to, he will lose exactly those qualities for which he is valued, and become as bitter and despairing as Matthew Antoine (this is painfully expressed in his angry, hurt complaint to his aunt about how she is helping "them" to break him down through humiliation; p. 76, l. 22 – p. 77, l. 9).

In the novel, then, escape is not seen in a positive light. It is presented as an act of cowardice leading to self-destruction, as a denial and rejection of commitment and love, and also as a submission to the racist structures of the South. The "*vicious circle*" (p. 159, l. 28 – p. 160, l. 5) of fear and despair among black men can only be broken by someone who refuses to submit to the pressures of the racist, segregationist South. This role falls to Jefferson. Grant comes to realize in the course of the novel that, for him, escape is not an option. Jefferson, on the other hand, who is denied the option of escape, can be taught to stand up straight at the very end, thereby offering an example of dignity and respect which can symbolize for others the strength to be found in refusing to run away (even symbolically by running away from one's humanity).

On a purely symbolic level, one of the final passages in the novel gives the reader a glimpse of a more positive, transcendent concept of escape, untroubled by fear or despair. After Jefferson's execution, Grant is sitting under a tree near Pichot's plantation house, and sees a butterfly flying away (p. 238, ll. 10–25). This moment symbolizes Jefferson's escape – his death. Freed of the pain and ignorance and suffering of his short and unfortunate life, and having gone to his death with a measure of dignity, self-respect, self-knowledge, and peace, Jefferson has broken free of the vicious circle – for himself at the very end, but also for those he left behind, the black quarter of Bayonne. He has shown them that the only valid escape from life can be found in a refusal to conform to the enforced, negative expectations of the racist hierarchy under which they live.

Death

Death is a major factor in the novel. It is present in the title, and the story is framed by death – the deaths during the robbery at the beginning, and Jefferson's execution at the end. Violence and death cast a shadow over the lives of the black people of Bayonne – not only in their fate when they try to escape, but also in their daily lives – the bar fight in Chapter 25 makes this clear enough.

The most interesting aspect of the theme of death in *A Lesson Before Dying* is the way it is instrumentalized. For the white community (best represented by Sheriff Guidry and the various fat, amused, contemptuous white men he has around him in different scenes) the execution of Jefferson is an exercise in punishment, retribution, and also in the assertion of white supremacy in a racist society. The opening trial chapter makes it clear that Jefferson's race and skin color play a huge role in his conviction. He becomes for the white authorities a kind of scapegoat figure, who they can make an example of; in a racist culture, the death of a white man must have as a consequence the death of a black man. This brutal enforcement of white supremacy supports the racist hierarchy by affirming white dominance and enforcing black submission.

But Jefferson's death is not only a matter of crime and punishment. For the black community, his significance as a scapegoat acquires another dimension: sacrifice. This is how Jefferson sees himself. He speaks of himself as a hog, being fattened for slaughter (p. 80, l. 31; p. 81, ll. 4–5). This is during one of the early visits; later on, the sacrificial aspect of Jefferson's position becomes apparent in the expectations that are focused on him. These expectations arise from what Miss Emma wants Grant to help him with – to walk to his death like a man. In the face of death, he is expected to transcend the color line and die as a human being, instead of just as an ignorant young black man who was in the wrong place at the wrong time.

This role is of central importance for the novel. Jefferson must achieve dignity in a society in which, for blacks, dignity is something which must be fought for. The essential inhumanity of the segregationist culture tries to deprive him of respect and dignity, and it is this which Grant is trying to help him achieve (or recover) before his death. In accomplishing this, Jefferson provides something more important than any material benefit for the black community; he becomes a symbol of hope in the face of crushing adversity.

Hope

Death, despite its looming presence in the novel, is not itself the central issue. It serves as the central motor of the plot – from the deaths during the robbery through to Jefferson's execution – and the impulse for the characters' actions and motivations. But what it means most, within the novel and to the reader, as well, is the promise of a better world; and not an abstract, faith-bound concept like Reverend Ambrose's Heaven, but a very real world in which simple humanity and respect transcend racist hierarchies and segregationist society. While being very specifically placed in a small town in Louisiana during the years 1948-49, the novel acquires a great universality through this theme of hope in the face of adversity and death.

This is directly addressed by Grant in one of the key chapters in the novel (Chapter 12, pp. 83–91). The complex theme of hope touches on many other themes in the novel, especially those concerned with racism and oppression, but also the roles of men and women and the themes of family and community. In Chapter 12 the theme of hope is addressed in a number of contexts: the old men in the bar enthusing about baseball and Grant's memories of the epic boxing matches between Joe Louis and Max Schmeling; James Joyce's short story "*Ivy Day in the Committee Room*" and the Irish lecturer who introduced Grant to it; and another execution, in Florida.

The African-American heroes of sport – baseball star Jackie Robinson and boxer Joe Louis – provide focal points for the hope of the community. Their distant star status elevates them above the day-to-day struggles and problems of the fans, but the identification with their race and achievements within a white-dominated society allows the fans to project their hopes onto these figures, and in return to share in their struggles and triumphs. The old men discussing Jackie Robinson in the Rainbow Club identify completely with their hero (p. 84, ll. 5–24), acting out great moments in his career, becoming the baseball player (p. 84, l. 7). Their enthusiasm reminds Grant of his own

Jackie Robinson

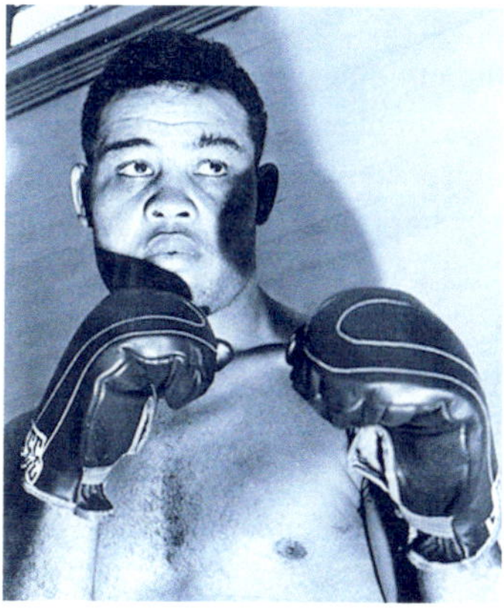

Joe Louis

childhood, listening to the boxing matches on the radio between Louis and Schmeling. After their first fight, which Louis lost, Grant can recall *"how depressed everyone was [...] For weeks it was like that. To be caught laughing for any reason seemed like a sin. This was a period of mourning. What else was there in the world to be proud of, if Joe had lost?"* (p. 84, l. 29 – p. 85, l. 4). A preacher even gives the competition between the two boxers a Biblical character, comparing them to David and Goliath.

The rematch between the two boxers is a big event, not just for Grant, as the people in the black quarter congregate around the two radios: *"I was seventeen then. I was not the youngest, nor surely the oldest. I was just one. Praying and hoping for the only hero we knew."* (p. 85, ll. 10–12). When Louis wins - *"Could God let it happen again?"* (p. 85, l. 17) - there is ecstatic chaos. Grant describes wild scenes of unrestrained joy. *"For days after that fight, for weeks, we held our heads higher than any people on earth had ever done for any reason"* (p. 85, ll. 23–24). The African-American boxer Joe Louis provided a clear and precise focal point for all the hopes of the black community, which is otherwise denied the means (or a reason) to celebrate one of their own: a source of hope and pride.

These two scenes are very specific to the African-American experience in the South during a particular, pre-Civil Rights Movement era. But Gaines now has Grant move on to another expression of the same theme of hope and pride, which gives the theme universal dimensions. Grant recalls an Irish lecturer who came to his (for blacks only) university while he was studying there. He is not sure how his university managed to engage a white lecturer, but the little man left a big impression on the narrator: his lecture is about Irish literature, *"Yeats, O'Casey, Joyce – names I had never heard before"* (p.85, l.33 – p.86, l.1), and about Parnell (an Irish nationalist who fought against British rule in the late 19th century). He then discusses James Joyce, in particular a story of his called *"Ivy Day in the Committee Room"* from the short story collection Dubliners. *"Regardless of race, regardless of class, that story was universal, he said"* (p.86, ll.8–9) – Grant is intrigued by this statement and manages to find a copy of the story in an anthology of short stories. At first he is disappointed - *"All I saw in the story was some Irishmen meeting in a room and talking politics"* (p.86, ll.24–25). But over time, with the story in the back of his mind, he comes to realize the truth of what Joyce wrote and the Irish lecturer said. There is a universality in the respect and adoration of the dead, in the way people from whatever race or class *"talked about the dead and about how great the dead had once been"* (p.86 ll.31-2). This is just as relevant for blacks in the segregationist South as it is for the oppressed Irish under British colonial rule. Like Grant, the reader is also brought to an understanding of the universality of a story which has been firmly placed in a specific time and place. When there is little hope to be found in the immediate realities of a life in a racist culture, hope can be focused on the great heroes, and once these heroes are dead and gone, the hope remains and even grows until the heroes, the great dead, acquire mythic proportions.

Grant's thoughts drift in this chapter on a course from the heroes of sport and past the Irish story to more pressing matters: *"But I was not thinking about Jackie now, or Joe Louis, or the little Irishman; I was thinking about that cold, depressing cell uptown"* (p.87 ll.2-4). Gaines draws a parallel here for Grant and for the reader, preparing the teacher and us for the full extent of what is expected of Jefferson in the way he approaches his own death. What follows also foreshadows the symbolic power Jefferson will come to embody: *"And my mind went back to that cell uptown, then to another cell, somewhere in Florida. After reading about the execution there, I had dreamed of it over and over and over.*

As vividly as if I were there, I had seen that cell, heard that boy crying while being dragged to that chair; 'Please, Joe Louis, help me. Please help me. Help me.' And after he had been strapped in the chair, the man who wrote the story could still hear him cry, 'Mr. Joe Louis, help me. Mr. Joe Louis, help me.' " (p.87, ll.23–30).

This section of the novel is a powerful and moving expression of the theme of hope. The young man who was executed doesn't call on an abstract, white man's God – he cries for help to a very real hero, a focal point of hope for black men, someone who had triumphed in a white man's world and had received all the love and hope of an oppressed people. Grant recognizes Jefferson in the character of the young man (p.87, ll.32–34): but by the end of the novel the roles and symbols will have become more complex, and it will be Jefferson who becomes a figure of hope to be called upon.

Heroes and myths

Grant's conversation with Jefferson about the hero as a focal point for a community's hope and as a way of breaking the myths ("*A myth is an old lie that people believe in*"; p.182, ll.27–28) brings together all the themes in the novel.

Grant defines a hero for Jefferson as "*someone who does something for other people*" (p.181, ll.28–29). This "*something*" is expected of Grant, but he cannot provide it; it is not expected of Jefferson (p.182, ll.8–11), and it is in this assessment of Jefferson's "*uselessness*" that his strength and potential as a hero and focal point for hope lies. Grant clearly states this: "*I want you to show them the difference between what they think you are and what you can be*" (p.182, ll.14–15). He acknowledges the limitations of his own role as teacher – that he is tolerated by the white authorities so that he can teach reading, writing and arithmetic – but "*nothing about dignity, nothing about identity, nothing about loving and caring*" (p.182, ll.19–20). It is important when looking at this passage to bear in mind the later conversation between Grant and Reverend Ambrose, during which Ambrose attacks Grant with a very similar argument (pp.201–206).

Without sinking to the depths Antoine reached in his frustration and self-hatred, Grant has come to understand his place in the system, and to recognize that he is not "hero" material. He lacks this "*something*" which a hero can provide for other people. The "*something*" is explained soon afterwards; it is that which is needed to destroy a myth. "*White people believe that they're better than anyone else on earth [...] The last thing they ever want is to see a black man stand, and think, and show that common humanity that is in us all*" (p. 182, ll. 28–31). He admits that he himself is not a threat to the myth of white supremacy, and neither is Reverend Ambrose – both of them have a role to play in society, and they play it, one of them dispensing basic education and the other basic religion – in both cases non-threatening, non-subversive, and with no intention or chance of rocking the boat. "*They're safe with me. They're safe with Reverend Ambrose. I don't want them to feel safe with you anymore*" (p. 183, ll. 1–2).

Here we can see how Jefferson's significance has changed for Grant. A few months previously he had been concerned about who Jefferson would appeal to, whether it would be baseball star Jackie Robinson (p. 87, ll. 32–34): and now it is Jefferson himself who, in the moment of death, will become the focal point for the hopes – the hero - of the community. Grant is humble before Jefferson now, acknowledging that what Jefferson is capable of and what he can provide for the community is vastly greater than what he himself can (p. 183, ll. 19–26). He tells Jefferson how important he can be to those who love him and to the black quarter in general, and Jefferson is moved to tears, because what Grant is telling him and expecting of him, even demanding of him, is not just a burden; it is a clear and unambiguous expression of need, love and belonging. Jefferson belongs to the community, and in his last moments they will support him with love as he in turn gives them back that "*something*" that only heroes can provide - hope and pride.

Jesus and Easter: sacrifice and salvation

Jefferson is to be executed shortly after Easter. Inevitably, this suggests the Crucifixion, and not only to Grant – Jefferson is not unaware of the significance of the date (even if he does at times get confused about what happened when; p. 131, ll. 9–23 and p. 208, ll. 21–26). Grant suspects that the date set for the execution was pushed back by two weeks in order to protect the *"sensitive few"* (p.150, ll.28–33; p.149 ll.13–21) from having to associate Jefferson's execution with the death of Jesus. But the connection is already there.

Jefferson has complained already about feeling like he is being fattened for slaughter – he thinks it is for Christmas, though (pp.80–81). Later, when he knows the date of his execution, he understands clearer what it means and what is expected of him. In the last conversation we as readers are shown between Grant and Jefferson (pp.207–213), Jefferson is shown in a new light. He has come to terms with his impending execution, it seems, and is also now clear in his mind what exactly is expected of him. He seems calmer. Less sullen, less angry, less likely to look with cynicism or hatred at his visitors. This change in his behavior can be explained in the context of Jesus, as well. What has obviously impressed Jefferson about the story of the Crucifixion is Jesus' uncomplaining acceptance of his fate. He mentions a couple of times, almost in admiration, that Jesus *"never said a mumbling word"* (p.131, ll.22–23; p.208, ll.25–26, and p.210, ll.30–32) when he was killed at Easter.

As his own understanding of the role he now embodies for the black quarter grows, so does his own ability to fill this role. He fully understands by this point (Chapter 28) how important it is that he stands up straight and defies the expectations of the racist authorities who have sentenced him to death. That he exemplifies the dignity, sense of identity and simple humanity that three hundred years of slavery and oppression have failed to completely destroy. This scene sees a reversal of Grant's and Jefferson's roles, with Jefferson offering the food (suggesting the breaking of bread in Christian rituals as much as it recalls the simple comfort provided by his godmother) and confronting Grant with hard, painful truths: *"I'm the one got to do everything, Mr. Wiggins. I'm the one. […] Me to take the cross. Your cross, nannan's cross, my own cross. […] Yes, I'm youman, Mr. Wiggins. But nobody didn't know that 'fore now"* (p.211, ll.12–32). His complaint that it is only at the moment of his death that anyone – even those who claim to love him – accepted him as a valid human being is fully justified. But instead of dwelling on the unfairness and injustice of his situation (which he has done enough of in his jail cell, only provoked out of depression by Grant's visits) he has now grown in stature to be able to fulfill the expectations placed in him. He is ready to shoulder a burden of sacrifice for the benefit of others, echoing the central message of the Crucifixion, he is ready to challenge the white supremacy by refusing to be the subhuman "*hog*" or "*nigger*" he is thought to be, and he is ready now to offer himself as a focal point for hope and pride, giving his godmother, Grant, and all the other people from the black quarter of Bayonne a symbol of hope closer to their own lives and realities than Joe Louis, Jackie Robinson, or Jesus Christ.

Coping with Exam Papers

Generally, tasks on texts, whether they are fictional or non-fictional, fall into three categories: 1) **comprehension**, 2) **analysis** and 3) writing a **composition** or a **personal comment**.

1. Comprehension

All comprehension tasks aim at finding out whether you have **understood** the novel. Usually you are given an extract and are asked to locate it within the framework of the whole novel. You must select the relevant events which lead up to the extract and which take place afterwards. When answering comprehension questions you should refrain from stating your own opinion, unless expressly asked to do so.

2. Analysis

Analysis tasks go beyond a simple understanding of the text. You may be asked to deal with the whole novel or to deal with the selected extract in detail. Analysis questions often concern language and imagery, characters, or the way the plot is structured. Here again, you should avoid giving your own opinion. Be careful not to retell the story: you really need to analyse what is happening on a more abstract level, e.g. don't just say what a character does, but explain why he or she does it, or find an adjective to describe the character, etc.

3. Evaluation

This area covers a wide range of different tasks. Indeed you may be offered a choice of two tasks.

You may be asked to write a **composition** or a **comment**, which often require you to show that you have understood what the intention of the story is. Tasks often deal with a general interpretation of the novel so make sure your ideas are plausible and well argued. This means that your ideas have to be in line with the novel and that you must always be able to prove what you say by referring to the stories. Never just make a supposition and leave it at that.

You may be asked to write a 'personal comment', which means you are obliged to give your own opinion, so make sure you base it on informed judgement, for which you need a thorough knowledge not just of the novel but also of the way it is constructed, so avoid making statements which you cannot prove.

Often you will be given the choice of doing a 'creative task'. Although at first this may seem easy, you should only choose to do a creative task if you have practised enough beforehand and your teacher seems happy with your work in this area. Creative tasks can involve:

- a change of perspective (i.e. recounting events or situations from the point of view of another character);
- reflection on other characters or events: this can often be in the form of a diary entry;
- filling in the gaps: here you might be asked to fill in what the reader does not learn directly from the text. This can often be in the form of a letter, an extra scene or an additional piece of dialogue.

Whatever kind of creative tasks are set, you must remember to stay within the context of the novel. This means that you must not simply fantasize but look, for example, at the way a certain character behaves.

Operative Words

Regardless of which category of tasks you are dealing with, it is extremely important to read the task carefully and look for the operative words, which tell you exactly what is required of you. Here is a list of common operative words, in alphabetical order. (They are not necessarily confined to comprehension, analysis or composition)

Analyse …: an analysis is a detailed examination of, for example, an important topic, the narrative technique, or one or more of the characters, so you must deal carefully with all the relevant aspects.

Assess …: here, you must consider in a balanced way the points for and against something.

Comment on …: here you are allowed to give your personal opinion on, say, narrative technique or the way characters behave, but you must always give evidence from the novel to support it.

Compare …: you must highlight similarities and differences, most frequently between characters and events. A similar kind of task is:

Contrast …: here, however, you should concentrate on the differences.

Describe …: in this kind of task you must show what something (e.g. setting) or somebody (one or more of the characters) is like by giving

a detailed account. Be careful not to forget any relevant details and choose examples from the text to illustrate the points you have made.
Discuss …: if you are asked to discuss a particular aspect of the novel (e.g. its narrative technique or the characters and how they interact), you should examine the issue from all sides before you state your personal opinion.
Evaluate …: here, you must form an opinion after carefully considering and presenting the advantages and disadvantages of a particular situation or course of action.
Examine …: this is another way of asking you to **analyse** something.
Explain …: this kind of task involves giving reasons for the action, characters' motives or how the specific use of certain techniques like the use of imagery or modes of description produce a certain effect.
Characterize/Describe somebody's character …: here you should describe the specific features of, most often, one or more characters, by looking at how they are presented and the way they speak.
Illustrate …: here, you have to make something clear by choosing relevant examples. Read the task carefully to find out whether you have to concentrate on the given passage or whether you may, or have to, refer to the whole novel.
Interpret …: here you should deal with both form and content and how they work together to create meaning.
Justify …: here you must argue why something should be done or some decision taken or why some conclusion was made.
Outline …: an outline is a general account of something. In other words in your outline you can re-tell the major events of a story, or give a brief description of a character, which includes only the very relevant elements only and omits all details.
Point out …: here, you must find and explain certain aspects of the text.
Present …: here, you are expected to write something down in your words.
State …: here, you are expected to specify clearly whatever is required. You may be required to state the main features of or development of something.
Summarize …: a summary is more precise than an outline. When writing a summary you should select the key points and ideas etc. and

structure them. As in an outline you should not go into detail or give examples. You might, for example, be asked to summarize a dialogue or argument, or the events of the whole novel or an extract.

General points to remember – or how to impress the examiner:

- You are not writing for yourself, but you are addressing the examiner(s) who will mark your work. Examiners are not mind-readers, so you must express yourself as clearly as possible.
- Always collect and organize your ideas before you start writing. In this way the examiner will be able to follow you more easily.
- When writing a composition or a personal comment, remember three simple steps: say what you are going to say – say it – sum up what you have said. Doing this will make your text more convincing.
- When you are dealing with literature you should always use the simple present tense when discussing characters and action.
- Structure your work by using '**connectives**' to link your ideas, so that the examiner can follow the presentation of your arguments. Otherwise he or she gets the impression that you are 'rambling'. You should be able to find a list of connectives in your coursebook.
- Likewise, avoid all forms of repetition, unless you want to return to a point you made earlier on. In this case you should use expressions like 'as I have already pointed out …'
- You can always impress the examiner by using suitable quotes, but they should only be used to **underline** a point you have already made or are going to make, and not instead of making a point – otherwise the examiner will think you are simply copying from the text or that you are unable to express yourself correctly. Always put your quotations in inverted commas. If you are allowed to use the book, you should also refer to the page and line of the quote.
- Usually the test paper will tell you how many words you have to write for each section of the test. If you have time after re-reading and checking your paper for coherence, mistakes, etc., try and count your words, as you may have marks deducted for writing too little or too much.

Written Test

Test

Ernest J. Gaines, *A Lesson Before Dying*
Excerpt from Chapter 23 (p. 176, l. 7 – p. 177, l. 25)

Tasks

1. **Describe the background to the excerpt.**
2. **Explain why Grant Wiggins "caught himself grinning" (p. 177, l. 16).**
3. **Imagine you are Paul at home with his wife that evening. How might he describe what happened?**

Dealing with the Test

1

This task requires you to describe what has happened before, so that the excerpt can be understood within the context.
What you do not want to do is describe the whole story. You should concentrate on those facts and events that are of relevance to this scene.
First of all, work out what the scene is about:

1. Why is Jefferson in prison? He was convicted of a murder he did not commit.
2. Why is Grant visiting him? He has been asked by Jefferson's godmother to teach him how to die like a man
3. How has Jefferson behaved up to this point? Jefferson has been unfriendly and uncooperative. He took the words of his lawyer that he is just a "hog" to heart, and refuses to behave like a human, rejecting the love of those around him. He has been aggressive to Grant.
4. How has Grant reacted to having to visit Jefferson? Grant is reluctant to help Jefferson. He cannot see how he can help him. He feels frustrated by his lack of success in getting through to Jefferson.
5. What other factors might be important to understand this excerpt? Grant gave Jefferson a radio, the first time someone

has done something for him, so Jefferson is a little more open than usual. The children of the parish collected nuts for Jefferson, which Grant gave him when he arrived on this visit.

Then put this information together in a coherent paragraph.

2

Here some analysis is required. For someone reading just this scene, Grant grinning because of a person saying thank you may seem very strange. Yet this scene is a key scene, as we see a small change in Jefferson, which marks his slow transformation.

Previously:

- He had acted as if he were just a hog with no human feelings.
- He had cruelly rejected the love and food of his aunt.
- He had refused to talk with Grant.

Now:

- He has thanked someone for doing something kind to him. The children gathered nuts just so he could have something pleasant to eat. This act of charity by others has been acknowledged by Jefferson. It is his first step on his way to becoming a man.

3

To deal with this task, you are required to do three things:

a) Understand what sort of person Paul is.

b) Retell part of the story from another perspective.

c) Recount much of what has happened in order to understand why Grant left the prison in a good mood.

a) Paul is the white deputy at the prison. We have learned that he is a sympathetic kind man who does not look down on blacks. This means that he can give a sympathetic account of what has been going on.

b) Paul obviously does not know about the details of the encounters between Grant and Jefferson. He is intelligent enough to be aware that they have not been going too well. So he can only recount his impressions.

c) Here, you can have Paul talk to his wife about previous visits, in which Jefferson's visitors left looking unhappy, or about Jefferson's state of mind (as a guard, he knows that Jefferson is sullen, depressed and uncooperative). This is the first time that he has seen Grant with a grin on his face. As Grant does not tell him what has happened, Paul must speculate about the possible reasons for his happiness.

When writing the dialogue, you will use a lot of phrases like "Grant must have …", "I suppose that …", "I wonder whether …", "Jefferson has probably …"